# Sport, Racism and Social M

Racist abuse may at one time have been hurled across the sports stadium or scrawled on a wall. But in today's social media world it can be published to millions, from almost anywhere, in an instant. *Sport, Racism and Social Media* provides the first significant, academic account of how social media is shaping the nature of racism in sport. Among the questions it addresses are:

- How, and why, is racism being expressed across different social media platforms and sporting contexts?
- To what extent is social media providing new platforms for traditional prejudices or actually creating new forms of racism?
- How can campaigners, authorities and individuals best challenge and counter these forms of racism?

Combining analysis of social media content with in-depth interviews with athletes, fans, campaigners and officials, and including extensive case studies of soccer, boxing, the NHL, the NBA and cricket, the book provides important new insights on a familiar but ever changing story. It is essential reading for any student, researcher, media professional, administrator or policy-maker with an interest in sport, new media or the issue of racism in wider society.

**Neil Farrington** is Senior Lecturer in Sports Journalism at the University of Sunderland, UK.

**Lee Hall** is Senior Lecturer in Journalism at the University of Sunderland, UK.

**Daniel Kilvington** is Associate Lecturer in Media at the University of Sunderland, UK.

**John Price** is Senior Lecturer and programme leader for BA (Hons) Sports Journalism at the University of Sunderland, UK.

**Amir Saeed** is an online tutor at the University of Leicester, UK and was until recently the Programme Leader of BA (Hons) Media, Culture and Communication at the University of Sunderland, UK.

# Routledge research in sport, culture and society

# Sport, Racism and Social Media

Neil Farrington, Lee Hall,
Daniel Kilvington, John Price and
Amir Saeed

Routledge
Taylor & Francis Group

LONDON AND NEW YORK

First published 2015
by Routledge

2 Park Square, Milton Park, Abingdon, Oxon OX14 4RN
711 Third Avenue, New York, NY 10017, USA

*Routledge is an imprint of the Taylor & Francis Group, an informa business*

First issued in paperback 2016

*British Library Cataloguing in Publication Data*
A catalogue record for this book is available from the British Library

*Library of Congress Cataloging in Publication Data*
Farrington, Neil.
Sport, racism and social media / Neil Farrington, Lee Hall, Daniel
Kilvington, John Price and Amir Saeed. – 1st edition.
    pages cm. – (Routledge research in sport, culture and society)
    1. Sports–Social aspects. 2. Racism in sports. 3. Social media.
    I. Hall, J. Lee, 1978– II. Kilvington, Daniel. III. Price, John, 1973–
    IV. Saeed, Amir. V. Title.
    GV706.5.F37 2014
    306.4'83–dc23                                            2014011031

ISBN 978-0-415-83986-0 (hbk)
ISBN 978-1-138-69538-2 (pbk)

Typeset in Times New Roman
by Wearset Ltd, Boldon, Tyne and Wear

# Contents

# About the authors

**Neil Farrington** was a multi award-nominated UK sports journalist with 18 years' experience of covering international, national and regional sport, including the Olympic Games and football World Cup. He is now a Senior Lecturer in Sports Journalism at the University of Sunderland.

**Lee Hall** is Senior Lecturer in Journalism at the University of Sunderland. He was formerly digital editor at the *Sunderland Echo* after a long spell working in magazines which included editing national newsstand video-games titles. He continues to write about the games industry for publications such as *Edge*.

**Dr Daniel Kilvington** is Associate Lecturer in Media at the University of Sunderland. His recent PhD analysed the reasons for the lack of Asian professional footballers playing in the UK today.

**Dr John Price** is Senior Lecturer and programme leader for BA (Hons) Sports Journalism at the University of Sunderland. He is a former regional newspaper journalist.

**Dr Amir Saeed** is an online tutor at the University of Leicester and was until recently the Programme Leader of BA (Hons) Media, Culture and Communication at the University of Sunderland. His research interests are in 'race', racism and Islamophobia.

# 1   Introduction

There has been an air of complacency about racism in sport. Take football, for example. While acknowledging that more needs to be done, the Fédération Internationale de Football Association (FIFA) recently boasted racism was 'on the decline', thanks in no small part to its own campaigns (FIFA 2011). In evidence to a parliamentary investigation into racism in football, the Premier League claimed arrests at football matches to be 'at a record low', with arrests for racist chanting forming 'a tiny percentage of the 13.4 million individual attendances over the course of the season' (Premier League 2012). The subsequent report by the Culture, Media and Sport Committee stated: 'The atmosphere experienced by those attending football matches has changed hugely since the 1970s and 80s when racial and other forms of abuse were common' (Culture, Media and Sport Committee 2012). And even Prime Minister David Cameron has expressed a view, saying: 'If everyone [in football] plays their role, then we can easily crush and deal with this problem' (BBC Online, 22 February 2012).

Some of these comments were undoubtedly made with public relations in mind. But their danger is that they seriously underestimate the nature and extent of the problem. Cutting the number of arrests, or reducing the number of incidents of racist abuse, is a long way from genuinely tackling racism in sport. First, the comments downplay the complex and varied nature of racism. As Lord Herman Ouseley, Chair of Kick It Out, has observed: 'While overt, in-your-face racism has been tackled in a way that has been tangibly managed, subtle or institutional racism is still a problem' (Farrington *et al.* 2012). Second, the comments ignore the pervasive, social nature of the problem. Reducing racist behaviour within and around football grounds falls far short of addressing the underlying attitudes that lead to such behaviour. As one campaign group explained to the parliamentary committee: 'Whilst there has been a change in behaviour at football matches, racist attitudes are still widely prevalent because racism remains a widespread problem in society' (SRTRC 2012). Similarly, former England and Liverpool footballer John

Barnes has said: 'If you're a racist, you're not going to change your mind because a club says it's wrong to be racist … ultimately, until we get rid of it [racism] in society, it will exist in all walks of society' (BBC Online, 22 February 2012).

To be fair to football and other sporting authorities, they can only do so much. The problem is one that also requires wider social measures and change. But the point here is that complacent statements about declining levels of racism, or being able to 'easily crush' the problem, actually make the issue more difficult to deal with. To ignore or underplay the problem is to add to the problem. It would be more accurate to say that racism has, to some extent, been managed by sporting authorities, rather than genuinely addressed. While overt racism may now be better policed and less socially acceptable within some sporting arenas, it has not gone away. Instead it has sought and found new outlets. One such outlet is social media – the focus of this book.

A recent international study of online hate speech concluded that the emergence of social media had led to a flood of extreme racist and other discriminatory material. It stated:

> New ways of using the web (such as social networking sites like Facebook and user generated content sites such as YouTube) have led to an explosion of online bullying and hate. Social networking sites are used to promulgate hate and extremist content, increasing the depth and breadth of hate material that confronts non-extremist users.
>
> (ICCA 2013: 7)

Among the examples cited in the report were Facebook groups called 'Hitting Women' and 'Join if You Hate Homosexuals'. The report's authors stated that social networking sites were making it easier for bigots to find people with like-minded views, and to air these views to a wider and often younger audience (ICCA 2013: 9).

Bartlett *et al.* (2014) conducted a study analysing the use of racial, religious and ethnic slurs on Twitter. Their findings suggest that approximately 10,000 uses of these terms are published on the platform each day. The most commonly used terms are White Boy, Paki, Whitey, Pikey, Coon, Nigga and Spic. While a large proportion of the terms are being used in 'non-derogatory' ways, such as to express in-group solidarity, the study estimate that around 2,000 tweets per day contain examples of directed racial or ethnic prejudice (Bartlett *et al.* 2014).

Kick It Out have reported seeing a 43 per cent rise in the number of complaints about discriminatory posts on social media in the last year. Director Roisin Wood said:

Social media is a massive issue. Sometimes people are using the force of social media to abuse players and to abuse other fans. These are very serious indications. We can only see that going one way and that's an increase.

(Herbert 2014)

In short, social media is providing an outlet for the mass publication and sharing of racist views and abuse. Sport has been a major focus for this content through the expression of racist views, the perpetuation of racist stereotypes and the targeted abuse of sports stars. The problem is significant and getting worse. In this book we seek to explore the nature and causes of the problem before offering some suggestions for the way forward.

To some extent the book takes a national focus in that it discusses cases, police and prosecution statistics relating to the UK. However, it also presents a wider perspective on the issue by exploring global issues relating to the management and control of social media, and by considering international examples from the worlds of cricket, football, the National Basketball Association (NBA) and the National Hockey League (NHL). This wider perspective is crucial to an understanding of the issues because, as we discuss, social media and its content are not constrained by national borders. Furthermore, in an attempt to address the complexities of the issues, we draw on ideas from a variety of academic fields including media and cultural studies, journalism, sociology, computer science and psychology. The book combines discussion of previous studies with new empirical research including content analysis and a range of interviews with athletes, sports administrators, journalists and academics.

In Chapter 2 we provide a critical discussion of the rise of social media, defining what we mean by social media and analysing the various forms it may take.

Chapter 3 explores issues relating to the management and control of social media, discussing criticisms of organisations such as Twitter and Facebook, and examining the problems faced by national authorities in policing content and prosecuting offenders on global platforms.

Chapter 4 discusses attempts to define 'race' and racism before looking to the field of social psychology for insights into the causes of racist behaviour. It then examines research relating to racism and the emergence of online and digital worlds.

Chapters 5 to 8 develop and apply ideas from earlier chapters to a series of case studies across different sports. They examine how and why social media has been used to publish racist content, perpetuate racist stereotypes and target racist abuse at fans and athletes. The sports analysed are football, cricket, boxing, basketball and ice hockey.

Chapter 9 seeks to draw together the book's key findings to present recommendations on the way forward. What are the main causes of the problems of sport, racism and social media? And how can they best be tackled? Where, and by who, does action need to be taken? And what are the obstacles that need to be overcome?

If there has been complacency in some quarters about racism in sport then the constant and often alarming noises on social media should provide a wake-up call. The voices of prejudice on social media need to be better challenged and tackled. This book takes up that challenge.

# 2   The rise of social media

## Introduction

What are 'social media'? Establishing a working definition of social media and considering which platforms we deem relevant to the issues raised in this book are key concerns of this chapter. We will also provide a critical context for the discussions and case studies which follow in subsequent chapters.

Social media is a relatively new term, but it has been argued that the concept dates back millennia. Consider the example of Roman politician and cultural observer Marcus Tullius Cicero. In the first century BC this prolific chronicler penned letters containing news from Rome which could take weeks to reach the far corners of the vast empire. Those letters were passed on via a network of connected friends, often copied and quoted in a spread which we might now refer to as 'viral' – certainly they were communicated through social networks rather than open public channels. This form of dissemination is therefore in some ways similar to what we see today online. Among the key differences between Cicero's news and the reportage of the modern era is the speed at which information travelled and the mediating technology (Standage 2013). Cicero commented on virtually every aspect of Roman life 2,000 years ago, including the quality of gladiatorial sport. When, from a twenty-first-century viewpoint, we consider how far published discourse has come since then it is clear that in some respects it has changed very little. Commenting on sport is no longer the preserve of a privileged, educated elite. But with the lowering of barriers to publishing, sportspeople, fans and journalists alike sometimes resort to commentary that belongs in another age.

**Defining social media**

As Fuchs (2014) points out, for some theorists all media can be labelled as 'social', whether or not they involve communication between individuals or an individual and a group. Aspects of society are present in all technological artefacts we use, it is argued, and cognition itself is a social activity. While this viewpoint might provide an interesting touchtone for academic discussion in other work, it implies too broad a frame of reference for the purposes of this book so we must narrow our sights. We need to fix on a workable definition of the term.

Fortunately other theorists offer a more precise view of what social media means. Clay Shirky sees it as a user-focused label with examples defined by their contrasting qualities to the traditional, print-focused publishing described as 'legacy media' by Jeff Jarvis. Social media are tools to 'increase our ability to share, to co-operate with one another, and to take collective action, all outside the framework of traditional institutions and organisations' (Shirky 2008). The result of this freedom to create and collaborate is content which ranges from the sublime – user-generated maps of electoral wrongdoings – to the ridiculous, in the form of humorous feline memes known as 'lolcats' (Shirky 2011).

Elsewhere social media is practically dismissed as a buzzword driven by user-generated content, itself an internet buzzword (Boyd 2009). For Van Dijck (2013) 'social media can be seen as online facilitators or enhancers of human networks – webs of people that promote connectedness as a social value'.

It would seem that definitions of social media are almost as numerous as the services launched under that umbrella term by tech firms seeking to emulate the success of the likes of Facebook. Certainly social media is an amorphous term. Its definition has shifted and been refined as the internet has evolved from a scientist's internal communications tool into a transformative influence in the lives of billions. The term has come to be synonymous with user generated content and the rapid dissemination of information by eyewitnesses. Social media have also been characterised variously as tools for freedom (Hebblethwaite 2014) and for repression or economic exploitation (Lovink 2008) as well as spaces that provide a 'vacuum for abuse' by ex-professional footballer Stan Collymore (2014).

Social media have been sometimes heralded as emblematic of the democratic nature of the web – democratic as least when it comes to publishing without the barriers endured and overcome by publishers in the pre-digital age. Others note that while social media can certainly be said to provide a means for almost anyone to broadcast to the masses, they certainly do not enrich the majority of users – in financial terms at least. Individuals who seek to make money from adverts placed on their content might aspire to become a 'YouTube sensation', but they are reliant on the fickle wind of virality to generate revenue, and even then it is typically a small slice of a much larger gain made by the new giants of the media landscape such as Google and Facebook.

The notion of social media as a facilitator of expression for the disenfranchised and a lever for change was popularised – largely, it must be said, thanks to mainstream media coverage – during the 'Arab Spring'. However, the debate about social media's role in the series of popular uprisings continues (Howard and Hussain 2013). Some, such as Kathleen Carley of Carnegie Mellon University in Pittsburgh, have questioned social media as a causal influence, stating: 'It told people to go here, to do this, but the reason was social influence, not social networking' (Reardon 2012). Others have questioned the efficacy of social media as a prompt for action (Lindsey 2013) in the context of the Arab Spring. Others have posed similar questions in the period of civil disorder in the wake of the shooting of Mark Duggan and subsequent mobilisation of communities seeking to redress any negative associations with social media through the #riotcleanup campaign (McDermott and Jaffray 2011).

Clearly we must understand the contexts of social media, their growth and use, a little better before fixing on our definition for the purposes of this study and pinpointing the platforms of most interest in the context of a discussion of race.

## Growing numbers

However they are viewed, social media are a potential gift to marketeers with qualities which make them appealing to those wishing to spread a personal message or monetise global followings. They are disruptive, immediate and present an opportunity to amplify messages with minimal effort and expense. In short, it's easy to understand the draw of social media for almost everyone including professional sportspeople keen to expand their influence, reputation and earning power. Social media certainly have the capacity to break down barriers between supporters and players. Discourse in this space is relatively free from controls and operates without much state intervention on a day-to-day basis. That freedom presents significant opportunities for expression, of course, but it also poses questions in terms of monitoring and policing for terms of abuse. Against this backdrop, and given such direct engagement between users, it is perhaps unsurprising that discourse can sometimes become unpalatable.

One particular appeal of social media – as opposed to more traditional media platforms – is the potential to connect with hard-to-reach demographic groups, usually younger people. But for those seeking to leverage social media reach, knowing which platforms to target is far from straightforward as the popularity of sites and services ebbs and flows under a number of influences. That is also an issue which poses challenges from an academic perspective. In October 2013, for instance, Twitter was hailed as a more popular network for teenagers than Facebook (Edwards 2013) prompting discussions of a possible shift in the social media landscape. But by as soon as early 2014 Twitter was under scrutiny when relatively depressing user numbers were published. The platform's longevity was questioned when quarterly user growth fell to its lowest levels since the network achieved mainstream popularity (Kang 2014). It should be noted that Twitter account registrations still rose by over 9 million in that three-month period, a number that still comfortably exceeded the total population of Greater London (7.7 million) at the same time. But in the digitally connected age of billion-user sites, the calibrations of how we measure success have been revised upwards to reflect rapid user growth and market penetration that would have been unthinkable a few decades ago.

The story of social media as we now know them can be traced to the beginning of connected communication in primitive forms optimised for the low bandwidth era of dial-up internet. Message boards and forums offered early opportunities for social interaction online at a time when the marketing of computer technology was morphing from a business-to-business proposition to a consumer electronics sell. The term 'social media' may not have been widely referenced in the pre-millennial dotcom era, but it works as a label for an increasing amount of online activity.

Social media may not have existed as a commonly accepted term until the mid-2000s, but it describes activity which can be tethered to social influence in any era, including Cicero's Rome. The idea that social media are a new phenomenon in the digital space is patently false. Some believe that post-dotcom bubble terms such as Web 2.0 and social media are merely attempts to rebrand internet functionality in the interests of major companies which had lost face with investors and the public. But there are simple reasons why that is a superficial summary of the situation and to consider that, while social media are not new, they are changing and growing in importance.

We must not veer too far in considering the influence of technological advances on our lives and end up in the trap of technological determinism. But it should be acknowledged that there are major changes which have contributed not only to a rise in social media use but a qualitative shift in the content – mainly faster connection speeds and the ubiquity of powerful, internet-enabled devices.

Social media remains a workable blanket reference to any online activity which involves engagement between an individual and groups of users who were not necessarily previously known to them. Historically, social media was essentially defined by what it did not represent than the nuances of myriad interactions it does encompass. Social media was something that took place online but was neither business-related nor media in the traditional form used as a communications tool by established publishing companies.

When the volume of all online activity multiplied, especially in the early 2000s, the small pockets of interaction had developed into a tidal wave of social connectivity. The growth in the internet as a social phenomenon was fuelled by advances in the amount of data that could be shared online quickly and a growing appetite for online communication. As people began to live more of their lives on the web, pastimes and practices previously seen as strictly limited to the physical world became available on the internet – from dating to shopping, playing games to filling out tax returns. The definition of social media barely shifted, but the volume of activity which fell within the bounds of the vague social interaction definition became so great that the terms were beginning to lose meaning.

After the millennium two factors helped to fracture the definition of what we now refer to as social media. First, the rise of blogging, which had started in the 1990s, powered by increasingly easy-to-use and predominantly free self-publishing software, meant legacy media companies began to lose their grip on the mechanisms for disseminating content. Second, the commercial battleground shifted from search to social. Google's victory in the former battle came through the leverage of scale. And it was scale that would win the social war too.

**Mapping social media**

For many, social media platforms are now trumping traditional media providers as the first port of call for information on unfolding events. Platforms such as Twitter offer – often in real-time – the potential to see, hear or read authentic coverage of escalating situations be they violent clashes between protesters and police, hastily deleted tweets from sportspeople or updates from a courtroom. Social media can present an unmediated version of events (Mason 2013) and comes in many forms. As we will outline later in this chapter – and as shall become clear in those which follow – there are many important social media platforms which are rarely mentioned – the likes of Pinterest, Instagram, LinkedIn and even Google+, to name some of the most populous. We have focused largely on the two most dominant networks – Facebook and Twitter.

If the major social media platforms were placed on a continuum from the least transparent to the most transparent in terms of accessing users' content, then Twitter would certainly be on the open end of that scale. While there is a mechanism for tweeting private messages using the direct message (DM) function, much of the discourse on Twitter is public.

Twitter is sometimes referred to as a micro-blogging platform. While users can opt to keep their updates private, very few do as the value in the service lies in the ease with which it can amplify messages to a wide audience who can easily share tweets. That streamlined functionality hastens the rapid spread of information. Tweets began as 140-character text-only messages which can include a link to web pages. But several services were established to enable users to attach a photograph to their tweet and subsequently video clips.

Twitter users can see a timeline of tweets from people they are following – which often includes re-tweeted messages, that is to say updates repeated with the Twitter username of the originator displayed, so that they are introduced to new people they may subsequently choose to follow. Users who build up a following on Twitter know their discourse will be exposed to those who effectively subscribe to their feed of tweets. For individuals and brands this has obvious appeal, especially for those wishing to communicate messages to wide audiences, often with a commercial dimension. For instance, celebrities – including sports stars – are incentivised to use Twitter to mention a product and there have been many instances of Twitter users harnessing the power of their brand to drive traffic to links via Facebook.

As with any medium, a whole class of experts and advisors offer tips on how to improve your following on Twitter – a space where insight as well as entertainment and controversy are likely to attract more followers. Twitter is not a platform for well-reasoned arguments or in-depth discussion, but its limits are what make it so convenient and therefore appealing. It is a space for pithy observation and breaking news flashes. And like so much media in the internet age, the greatest problem for those seeking to build a following is discoverability. The transient nature of a platform where tweets can be swallowed in a split-second by messages from other people you follow makes it hard to stand out. Repeating messages is considered counterproductive as this tends to result in users opting to 'unfollow' you as you are deemed to be spamming their timeline. The key to cracking discoverability is often achieving re-tweets – that way you can continually appear on timelines without looking like you are forcing the issue. The added benefit here being that you are seen as insightful and influential if you are re-tweeted, which only adds to your cache and increasingly the likelihood of others following your account.

Facebook is perhaps the most intimate social network, charting as it does details of people's everyday lives but also major events. It is the most populous social network with well over one billion users. The network's ubiquity has been challenged in recent years, but Facebook's propensity to survive and thrive where many other networks have been less successful is impressive. Their willingness to make multi-billion dollar acquisitions of services such as photo-centric user-generated content service Instagram and instant messaging offering WhatsApp mean they often absorb competitors thanks to their huge financial firepower. But the firm continues to innovate and challenge other competitors with equal muscle. The addition on a trial basis in January 2013 of Facebook Graph Search, which rolled out as a fully-supported feature in July, brought Facebook into competition with traditional search engines. Facebook's move into search may be a reaction to long-stated aims of monetising an enviable database of user information, but it is also a response to a shift in the opposite direction by search engine giant Google. Ever since in 2011 the company's visionary CEO Eric Schmidt predicted a 'social, local, mobile' future, Google has made high-profile moves to enter the social space. Google+ launched in 2011 and has grown to a membership of 500 million users, of whom around half are active.

For all the scorn poured on the notion of 'friendship' in this space, Facebook is a place of reciprocated intimacy. While users may not have 300 'friends' in their life offline, many Facebook users share details of their relationship status, state of inebriation and views of their employers to such a number through posts on the social network. The addition of support for photographs and videos has only made the window into people's lives provided by the network more vivid. With the ability to tag other users in Facebook, it is also possible for people to be portrayed in a flattering light as those who are connected to the subject can label them in content they share to their own friends.

## Using social media

There has been a great deal of research into the way behaviours change when individuals use the internet and a number of studies have focused on individual social networks. The mechanism of increasing influence through expanding your following on Twitter, for instance, provides an interesting talking point for those wishing to understand the psychology of social media use and the reasons why people make the comments they do to those in their network.

There is clearly a performative element to all social media. Every time someone posts a happy family photo of their beautiful children on Facebook they seek to convey a managed message to friends about their existence. Narcissistic behaviour and social media use seem to go hand in hand. Twitter is perhaps even more performative as the reward for entertaining people in that space is often more followers and therefore more influence.

In this book we will explore discourse involving sports stars, journalists and members of the public which involve racial epithets. In the background of our discussion lurks the question of why people make racially-charged comments on social media. Is their discourse heartfelt, or is the mediation of the platforms an amplifying or distorting force? Given the very public nature of some of the platforms we discuss – notably Twitter – it is difficult to understand why sports stars and fans in the gaze of the media and the law should make racist comments which can prove so costly. Research into the practice of 'trolling', the act of repeatedly making inflammatory – and often off-topic and offensive – comments via social media has suggested a link between bad behaviour online and narcissism. One recent study joined a list of others that linked trolling with sadism, psychopathy and Machiavellianism, concluding that 'cyber-trolling appears to be an Internet manifestation of everyday sadism' (Buckels *et al.* 2014).

One of the key objectives of this book is to further our understanding of this behaviour in the context of race. As we seek to comprehend the motives behind racist discourse we are effectively wrestling the question of the extent to which social media provides a mirror to users and how much it is influencing the users. Such is the significance of social media, some argue (Hinton and Hjorth 2013: 2), the phenomenon is altering the definitions of 'social' and 'media'. Hinton and Hjorth contribute to this discussion with their explanation of 'intimate publics'. This theory suggests that social and mobile media are forging social and cultural intimacies beyond the traditional intimacies triggered by physical proximity and familial ties. These cultural intimacies exist when individuals with no apparent connection find themselves united by a common passion. And there are few better examples of a public intimacy which can transcend barriers such as language and kick-start a conversation on a train than opining about sport.

Given the pervasive nature of social media, it is hardly surprising that interpersonal connections based on public intimacies are seen so frequently online. In fact, a driving mechanic of networks such as LinkedIn and Facebook is 'groups'. To suggest these groups are all collectives of individuals with a deep cultural intimacy would be to misunderstand the ubiquity of group membership and the diverse reasons groups are formed in this space. Groups and pages are formed to celebrate a favourite childhood chocolate bar or to petition for a statue of movie character Robocop to be built in Detroit. But even the most flippant groups act as micro communities and are used as a signal to people to find like-minded individuals.

Of course, we should not forget – given the ubiquity of platforms such as Facebook – that belonging to a social network or using social media tools is itself a form of cultural intimacy. Certainly one could reflect on the story of Facebook and perceive a tipping point when people stopped asking if you were on Facebook and were simply surprised if you were not. That is the kind of penetration to which rising social media networks aspire. In fact, Facebook is now so much the norm that not belonging to social networks has been raised as a cause for concern by some human resources departments (Hill 2012).

Social media tools such as Instagram and Twitter are especially interesting in the context of public intimacies when it comes to sport and fans' relationship with sporting professionals. The increasing distance between the public and players has long been bemoaned (Price *et al.* 2012) resulting in frequent attempts for sports professionals to seek to repair their relationship, work in their community and 'reach out to fans'. The old-fashioned intimacy enjoyed by football players and supporters who rode the same train to a match and enjoyed a drink in the same pub afterwards is all but forgotten in the modern era of £250,000 weekly salaries – with a few exceptions which are so rare they become news (Sharma 2013).

Social media is frequently trumpeted as a means to redevelop intimacy between players and supporters in a way which encompasses both the public intimacy of an apparently shared cultural background and in a far more traditional manner. In a space where fans, players and officials can communicate directly it is perhaps little wonder that all discourse is far from complementary. But brands – be they attached to individuals or organisations – can ill-afford to ignore social media's promise of wider influence and access to the lifestreams of consumers.

It is this contrast between the value to individual and institutional brands of a connected audience which seems to keep social media alive in sport. While some are so hurt by abuse in this space they quit social media altogether, others make high-profile errors of judgement and some even commit criminal offences using this technology. Yet almost no-one within sport wants to hit the 'off switch' and prevent social media engagement. Like the debate surrounding the right to freedom of expression, which is so often referenced as mitigation by those at the centre of a social media controversy, the fear is that banning employees from social media is akin to throwing the baby out with the bathwater.

## Focusing on social network services

One challenge when studying social media is reconciling our urge to organise and categorise platforms with the amorphous nature of the services themselves on the one hand and the emergence of new platforms on the other. Change is not only a factor influencing social media platforms, it is fundamental to how they survive and thrive. Hard-wired into the digital DNA of services such as Facebook, in the strings of code which form their makeup, is the means to augment and alter the services. Programmers are encouraged to create new functionality and find new ways of connecting Facebook to other websites and services by accessing a development platform to, say – at a basic level, enable users to log into a site and make comments automatically if they are signed into the social network. This single sign-in functionality may not materially alter the platform, but it contributes to the ubiquity of Facebook. As the tentacles of Facebook spread and recede the importance of the platform and its functions change, rendering it difficult to pin down for academic scrutiny.

Attempts to categorise social media are further complicated by the fact that there is a tendency for people to explore and exploit the tools at their disposal to find new and often unintended ways to use them. Emergent functionality is a term which describes our desire to find ways to exploit platforms in ways which were not intended by their creators. Often emergence is a goal of software developers, seen most obviously in the increasingly connected world of videogames where emergent gameplay is seen as a gold standard of development and a significant phenomenon worthy of study (Pearce *et al.* 2009). The aim is to enable players to immerse themselves in the mechanics of play beyond the scripted gameplay prescribed by the developers. The highest profile example of this in recent years is the phenomenon of Minecraft, though the potential for emergent gameplay underpins the appeal of older platforms such as World Of Warcraft and Second Life. The example of DayZ – a user-created spin-off of tactical shooter ARMA 2 – shows the possibilities of a connected community, open code and a desire to find emergent functionality. The game – essentially created by player and skilled programmer Dean Hall as a 'mod' – eventually became a standalone product.

Notwithstanding those challenges of defining social media, there are some critically accepted brackets within which we can place the various social media services. On the one hand, the likes of Facebook, Twitter and Google+ can be labelled social network sites (SNS) and on the other, services such as YouTube, Instagram and Pinterest are user generated sites (UGS). There are other categories concerning trade, such as eBay, and games, such as Farmville, as succinctly outlined elsewhere (Van Dijck 2013).

In this book we are focusing predominantly on the SNS category of social media. We are accepting an academically narrow definition of social media, focusing on the platforms which are most popular with sports stars, journalists and fans. We are unashamedly focusing on the platforms most likely to feature discourse which is relevant to discussions of race and racism, and where discourse is most likely to resonate by impacting on significant numbers of people. That is partly why we will also – in chapters about boxing, the NBA and NHL particularly – cover some user generated sites. We are going where the people are, fully aware that the conversation will almost certainly shift to new social media platforms, conscious that previously crucial plaforms such as Friends Reunited and MySpace are of limited relevance today.

We have to acknowledge that this is a somewhat anglophone-centric approach to the subject matter. Some of the largest social networks in the world have been omitted from our discussion, including China-only service Qzone, which is estimated to be third only to billion-user sites such as Facebook and YouTube in terms of active visitors with 712 million as of November 2013 (Smith 2013). Other China-only sites make the top 20 most populous networks in the world ahead of more familiar names in the West such as Foursquare, Vine and poster site for the dotcom era MySpace. Video broadcast sites Youku (175 million active users per month) and Tudou (114 million) and even Facebook-like RenRen (54 million) are still more populous than Pinterest (50 million).

We have avoided them for three key reasons: pure practicality, issues of cultural contexts and also regulatory contexts. There are differing laws surrounding freedom of expression around the world and varying appetites for attempting to control the information accessed by citizens, both of which naturally extend to the digital space. And while China's near-total ban on accessing Facebook has proved impossible to enforce (Macmillan 2012), a discussion of that country's social media landscapes demands more dedicated space elsewhere. We do explore cultural context in this book in our discussion of race, preferring to focus our attention on countries where cultural resonances are more familiar to the authors. And on a purely practical level there is the consideration of nuanced language and the sheer volume of content to cover in a discussion of the entire world's social media.

We opened this chapter by labelling social media an 'amorphous' term. As technologies advance and bandwidths expand, that description will become ever more pertinent. Social media has emergent functionality, in other words it can be used for purposes other than those originally intended. As we head towards Facebook's two billionth user account, people are finding new ways to exploit social media. For these reasons the definition of social media can never be fixed, we must only offer a snapshot which is sufficiently broad to resonate for some time to come, yet precise enough to enable a focused examination of some of the most worrying, uplifting and academically intriguing aspects of the phenomenon.

In truth, no anglophone social media platform has been ignored. Rather a guiding principle of seeking examples to aid our understanding of issues of race and racism in the social media space is one way which guides most researchers in one or another: impact. We are going where the people go, seeking to record and understand discourse of significance to our subject whenever it occurs. That's why many of our examples come from Twitter, a platform favoured by journalists who amplify controversies in that space with the aid of traditional media platforms. Twitter, a platform where public and private intimacies are deliberately blurred. This book was never intended to be, nor has it become, all about Twitter, but the platform provides an irresistible window for academics seeking to understand issues of race and the effects of technological tools.

# 3    Managing social media

## Introduction

Some of the most attractive characteristics of social media also provide some of its potential challenges for societies. It offers freedom of expression, but this comes with a steady flow of content which many people find unpleasant or far worse. It offers us the chance to connect and communicate with others, but with new friends and confidantes come potential critics and menaces. It offers some a cloak from oppressive regimes and others the playfulness of new identities, but with these benefits come the potential dangers of behaviour free of accountability. How best to weigh-up these tensions is an issue faced by authorities throughout the world. For some libertarians, freedom should rule and we should embrace the benefits of social media while just living with the downsides. For those who wish to oppress, social media is either a tool for snooping on their citizens or a threat that needs to be monitored and censored. For most though, the answer will lie somewhere in between these positions. This chapter seeks to explore the arguments that lie 'in-between'.

This chapter examines how relevant organisations and authorities have sought to regulate, police and prosecute racism on social media, discussing some of the problems they have faced in doing so. The material discussed is based on official documents, media content, interviews and content obtained through Freedom of Information requests to relevant organisations. The chapter begins with a discussion of how social media organisations deal with issues of racism and discrimination on their sites. It then goes on to examine how the police have responded to the benefits and challenges of social media, before finishing with an analysis of how prosecuting authorities are dealing with social media content.

## Social media organisations

As stated above, social media organisations are in a position of having to strike a balance between offering a platform for free discussion and offering some protection for people from abusive or harmful content. To some extent, whatever position they take, they will be criticised from one side or another – from those who think they regulate too much, and those who think they fail to do enough. So what do they do at present?

Twitter's official policy is that it will only investigate reports of abuse if they are reported by the victim or their authorised representative. In general, it advises users to notify their local police if they have a complaint about abusive content, claiming websites lack the powers to deal effectively with such cases. Its website states:

> If someone has Tweeted a violent threat that you feel is credible, contact law enforcement so they can accurately assess the validity of the threat. Websites do not have the ability to investigate and assess a threat, bring charges or prosecute individuals. If contacted by law enforcement directly, we can work with them and provide the necessary information for their investigation of your issue.
>
> (Twitter Help Centre – Reporting Abusive Behaviour)

Twitter does not screen content or remove potentially offensive or controversial content unless it breaches its 'Twitter rules'. These rules state that users cannot pose direct or violent threats, targeted abuse or harassment. However, the rules do not explicitly mention racism or other forms of discrimination. The website states:

> Twitter is a social broadcast network that enables people and organizations to publicly share brief messages instantly around the world. This brings a variety of users with different voices, ideas and perspectives. Users are allowed to post content, including potentially inflammatory content, as long as they're not violating the Twitter rules. It's important to know that Twitter does not screen content or remove potentially offensive content.

Twitter states it may warn users or suspend their accounts if it finds a breach of its Twitter rules. However, for many critics, it does not do enough to tackle the problem of people receiving racist and other forms of abuse. The organisation came in for particular criticism after a deluge of threats were issued to women campaigning for a female face to be included on UK bank notes. Campaigner Caroline Criado-Perez received hundreds of abusive messages, including bomb and rape threats, after the announcement that a picture of Jane Austen would appear on the new £10 note.

Following the threats, Andy Trotter, head of the Association of Chief Police Officers communications advisory group, said:

> While we do work with Twitter on some matters, I think there is a lot more to be done. They need to take responsibility, as do the other platforms, to deal with this at source and make sure these things do not carry on. They need to make it easier for victims to report these matters and, from a police perspective, they need to know that they can report these things to us.
>
> (BBC Online 29 July 2013)

Critics argue that Twitter, and other social media organisations, should take more responsibility for the nature of the content on their sites and make it easier for users to report threatening and illegal material. Such criticism provoked Twitter's UK general manager Tony Wang to apologise to the victims in the above mentioned case and admit that Twitter needed to do more to prevent abuse of its users. More than 140,000 people signed an online petition urging Twitter to add an online abuse button to tweets. Such a report function was recently introduced and attached to each message, allowing users to flag up potentially illegal content. However, this function takes users to a lengthy online report form which needs to be completed for each tweet. For the critics, this is not enough. Ms Criado-Perez said:

> Twitter's 'report abuse' button goes through to the old reporting form. What we're looking for is an overhaul of the system which sits behind the button. Right now, all the emphasis is on the victim, often under intense pressure, to report rather than for Twitter to track down the perpetrator and stop them.
>
> (BBC Online 3 August 2013)

Facebook has a more streamlined means of reporting content. Every page, photo or group on the site has a reporting tool next to it that can be used to send a report. Facebook says it reviews these reports and promises to remove any content which infringes its community terms. When users sign up to use Facebook, they are asked to agree to use their real identities and abide by these community terms. The terms relating to potentially racist content include the following:

- You will not post content that: is hate speech, threatening, or pornographic; incites violence; or contains nudity or graphic or gratuitous violence.

- You will not use Facebook to do anything unlawful, misleading, malicious, or discriminatory.

Facebook also provides users with the following advice in its section on community standards:

> Facebook does not permit hate speech, but distinguishes between serious and humorous speech. While we encourage you to challenge ideas, institutions, events, and practices, we do not permit individuals or groups to attack others based on their race, ethnicity, national origin, religion, sex, gender, sexual orientation, disability or medical condition.
>
> (www.facebook.com/communitystandards)

Like other social media sites, Facebook must try to find a balance between allowing users to publish and discuss controversial material in the spirit of free speech, while offering some protection against discriminatory or potentially harmful content. In fact, Facebook has received criticism for insisting users provide their real identities as some feel this inhibits communication, while endangering the safety and liberty of users living under authoritarian regimes. The site has also received criticism for not providing enough protection, particularly for its younger users, against online bullying and potentially harmful content. Prime Minister David Cameron was among those who criticised the site for showing footage of beheadings, describing it as 'abhorrent' on his Twitter feed. Facebook responded by saying it would take a more 'holistic' view of such content, removing material that glorified violence and insisting that violent content which was published on the site was accompanied by suitable warnings.

On the issues of harassment and abuse, Facebook states:

> Facebook does not tolerate bullying or harassment. We allow users to speak freely on matters and people of public interest, but take action on all reports of abusive behavior directed at private individuals. Repeatedly targeting other users with unwanted friend requests or messages is a form of harassment.

But for many, this is not enough. A recent survey of 10,000 13–22-year-olds found that 70 per cent of youngsters had experienced cyber-bullying and that one in five described this bullying as 'extreme'. The report also found that young people were twice as likely to be bullied on Facebook as on any other social media sites. Of young Facebook users, 54 per cent said that they had experienced bullying on the site, compared to 24 per cent on Twitter and 21 per cent on YouTube (Ditch the Label 2013).

The report was produced by anti-bullying charity Ditch the Label. Its authors called for social media companies to invest more in moderating content and to be more transparent about the levels and nature of bullying online. Liam Hackett, founder of Ditch the Label, said:

> Social media outlets have a massive duty of care to teen users. They are already doing a lot but more investment needs to be put into the resources of moderation ... What we believe social networks should have to do is produce an annual external audit which would measure cyberbullying activity on a network, how many people are reporting cyberbullying and what happened as a result, and we believe that those reports should be made public.
>
> (Evans 2013)

In the meantime, the impression given by social media organisations is that they will respond and act on this matter when they feel they have to, rather than taking the more proactive approach that anti-bullying campaigners, such as those cited above, have called for. That said, it must be acknowledged that such sites face a number of genuine problems in attempting to address these issues. A number of these challenges were identified in the recent international taskforce report on internet hate produced by the Inter-parliamentary Coalition for Combating Anti-semitism (ICCA 2013), and included:

- Challenge of scale – the huge amount of content posted on social media sites each day.
- Challenge of knowledge – the difficulty in judging what amounts to hate speech in different contexts.
- Challenge of politics – the difficulty adjudicating between the competing claims of political groups.
- Challenge of transparency – the volume of complaints makes it difficult to respond to individual reports.

The official policies of both Facebook and Twitter state that they will co-operate with US and non-US law enforcement agencies provided these authorities properly follow the legal proceedings. The following section will examine how police, particularly in the UK, are engaging with social media on these matters.

## Policing social media

The police are increasingly using social media as a promotional and operational tool. Of UK police forces, 98 per cent have an official Twitter feed with an average of 18,000 followers, while 96 per cent have a Facebook account and 94 per cent have YouTube accounts (Bartlett *et al.* 2014: 13). These accounts are mainly used to publicise police successes, provide warning and reassurance, and to issue information to the public.

Staffordshire Police has been identified as one of the forces leading the way in its use of social media and it was recently named as a case study of good practice by Facebook. David Bailey, Communications Manager at Staffordshire Police, said:

> We see our Facebook pages as a partnership with the communities, we have the main force page with around 47,000 fans across the county, but we also have pages like Staffordshire Horsewatch, which help bring together communities who share a specific interest, who then share information with each other and the force to help us all work together to reduce crime. Every comment made on our pages is read, we are listening to the views of our communities and it continues to provide a way for local people to help support their local officers. Our followers regularly share appeals and updates with their own friends about incidents that are happening.
>
> (The Sentinel 2013)

However, social media also provides police with a host of new challenges. In particular, the issue of internet trolling poses a problem of resources for many police forces. Lincolnshire Police revealed that they had experienced 3,437 incidents of trolling since 2009 (Bartlett *et al.* 2014). While the Metropolitan Police has said that around 2,000 crimes involving internet abuse are being reported to the police in London each year (BBC Online 19 September 2013).

Craig Mackey, Deputy Commissioner of the Metropolitan Police, says that dealing with social media offences has now become a day-to-day part of the force's activities. He identified two of the key problems faced by police in tackling the issue. One is the problem of offenders hiding their identity in order to evade prosecution. He said: 'Increasingly there is a trend for the person targeting someone to use false IDs and profiles and increasingly to use software which disguises their IP address which provides some challenges in what we do' (Bienkov 2013). Another difficulty for police is obtaining suitable evidence to provide a successful prosecution. He said: 'We need to provide screenshots from victims' digital media. It doesn't always provide the best evidence and we can later sometimes find some problems further down the line with the courts in trying to provenance things' (Bienkov 2013).

We issued a series of freedom of information (FOI) requests, asking police forces in the UK about the number of racially aggravated social media offences they had to deal with last year. The results revealed some significant differences in the way data is collected, the problems facing different forces and the way they are responding to the challenge. Lancashire Police reported that they had recorded 25 racially aggravated incidents in 2012 and only one of these had resulted in some form of police resolution (either caution, warning or criminal charge). In contrast, of 15 such incidents recorded by West Midlands Police, 13 resulted in police resolution. The force which officially reported the highest number of cases was West Mercia, with 25 crimes recorded. Five of these were resolved.

One thing that is clear from the data is that the number of 'race' related incidents dealt with by police amounts to just a tiny fraction of the racist content appearing on social media. This is acknowledged by True Vision, a website produced by the Association of Chief Police Officers on the subject of hate crime. It advises that:

> While you may come across a lot of material on the internet that offends you, very little of it is actually illegal. UK laws are written to make sure that people can speak and write, even offensive material, without being prosecuted for their views. Parliament has tried to define laws in a way that balances our freedom of expression with the right to be free from hate crime.
>
> (True Vision 2014)

According to the site, racist material that may be classed as illegal could fall into one of the following categories:

- Content that threatens or harasses a person or group of people based on 'race'.
- Content that stirs up hatred on the grounds of 'race'.
- Content calling for racial violence.
- Content that glorifies violence on the basis of 'race'.

While acknowledging that much hateful content will not be illegal, the police advise online users to report material they find offensive to the relevant website administrators. Such material, although often not unlawful, may not be allowed under the site's user guidelines and so may be removed. However, as we have seen in the discussion above, many people have concerns about the strictness, speed and effectiveness of sites, such as Facebook and Twitter, in responding to such complaints.

If users feel the content may be illegal, the advice is for them to contact their local police force. The next potential stage is a decision over whether or not to prosecute – which will be the subject of the following section.

## Prosecuting social media

This section will focus on issues around prosecuting social media content in the UK. However, it must be acknowledged that such issues exist in the shadow of US law on this matter. Across the world there exists a wide spectrum of laws on hate speech, ranging from national laws which are very restrictive of such speech to those which prioritise the protection of free speech. US law sits at the free speech end of this spectrum and this is significant both legally, because much social media content sits on US based servers, and philosophically, because this American tradition influences the thinking of key people in this debate. As Professor Jeff Rosen states:

> The reason why it is important to understand the American free speech tradition is that the ... executives who regulate speech are marinated in the American free speech tradition; they embrace it and accept it. In applying community guidelines ... which allow the regulation of hate speech and prohibit speech that promotes terrorism these executives are actually construing this through the narrow lens that there has to be some threat of imminent violence for the speech to be suppressed.
>
> (ICCA 2013)

It is in this light that the following discussion of UK legal proceedings needs to be viewed. In the UK, prosecutions of social media content are most commonly done through Section 127 of the Communications Act 2003, which makes it an offence to use public electronic communications networks to send grossly offensive messages. Charges brought under this section of the act rose from 498 in 2007 to 3,108 in 2012. However, these figures include a variety of offences and racist communications account for a relatively small proportion of the total number. In 2012, of the 3,108 charges brought under the act, 125 were for crimes flagged as being racially related. This is only 4 per cent of the total figure.

The other most commonly used law to deal with offences of this kind is the Malicious Communications Act 1988. There were 1,321 charges brought under this legislation in 2012. Of these, 63 were flagged as race hate crimes. This is 5 per cent of the total figure.

If we combine the figures we see that there were 188 criminal charges brought for racially aggravated offences in 2012. This amounts to 4 per cent of the 4,429 total number of charges brought under the two acts in that year. Based on the evidence presented in previous chapters, the number of cases being charged represents a small fraction of the racist content being posted on social media. For example, Bartlett *et al.* (2014) estimate that there are around 2,000 tweets a day containing potentially illegal racist content – that amounts to nearly 730,000 posts each year. While this is a global figure, the number of prosecutions appears miniscule in comparison.

While the number of racially related charges remains a relatively small percentage of the total figure, there has been a recent and significant increase in the number of charges brought. In 2008, there were 111 racially aggravated charges brought under the acts identified above. By 2012, this number had risen to 188 – an increase of around 70 per cent (above figures based on the FOI request to the Crown Prosecution Service).

These figures are likely to change again after the Crown Prosecution Service issued new guidelines relating to the prosecution of communications using social media. The guidelines state that cases falling into one of the following three categories should be prosecuted 'robustly':

1   Credible threats of violence.
2   Cases amounting to harassment or stalking.
3   Breaches of a court order, such as contempt of court or naming the victim of a sexual offence.

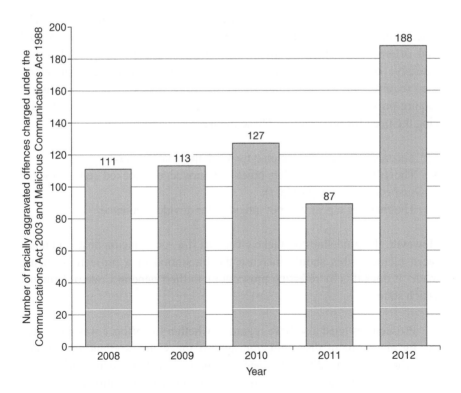

*Figure 3.1* Number of racially aggravated charges.

The guidelines then refer to a fourth category of communication involving posts deemed 'grossly offensive, indecent, obscene or false'. They state that cases of this kind are likely to have a 'high threshold' for prosecution and that in many cases prosecution is unlikely to be in the public interest. The effect of these new guidelines is to reduce the likelihood of people being prosecuted for something that they have posted on social media. The guidelines themselves acknowledge this, citing freedom of expression as the reason. They state:

> Every day many millions of communications are sent via social media and the application of section 1 of the Malicious Communications Act 1988 and section 127 of the Communications Act 2003 to such comments creates the potential that a very large number of cases could be prosecuted before the courts. Taking together, for example, Facebook, Twitter, LinkedIn and YouTube, there are likely to be hundreds of millions of communications every month. In these circumstances there is the potential for a chilling effect on free speech and prosecutors should exercise considerable caution before bringing charges.

The new guidelines acknowledge that communications on social media take place within a specific context and often involve exchanges that some would find offensive in other environments. They state that 'banter, jokes and offensive comments are commonplace and often spontaneous'. Therefore, they require that a post is more than 'offensive, shocking or disturbing' to require prosecution. The guidelines also list a series of factors further reducing the need for prosecution. These include:

- The suspect showing remorse for what they have posted.
- The offending post being quickly removed or blocked (either by the suspect or service provider).
- The fact that a post was not intended for a wider audience.

However, the guidelines do make clear that if a social media post contains a racist element, this should increase the likelihood of a prosecution being made. It does this by referring prosecutors to their general Code of Conduct which states:

> Prosecutors must also have regard to whether the offence was motivated by any form of discrimination against the victim's ethnic or national origin, gender, disability, age, religion or belief, sexual orientation or gender identity; or the suspect demonstrated hostility towards the victim based on any of those characteristics. The presence of any such

motivation or hostility will mean that it is more likely that prosecution is required.

These final guidelines were published following a three-month public consultation period. Among the 59 contributors to this discussion were the Football Association and Newcastle United Football Club.

Following the publication of the final guidelines, Keir Starmer QC, Director of Public Prosecutions, said:

> I believe the guidelines do set out the right approach to prosecution by making the distinction between those communications that should be robustly prosecuted, such as those that amount to a credible threat of violence, a targeted campaign of harassment against an individual or which breach court orders, and those communications which may be considered grossly offensive, to which the high threshold must apply.
>
> These are cases that can give rise to complex issues, but to avoid the potential chilling effect that might arise from high numbers of prosecutions in cases in which a communication might be considered grossly offensive, we must recognise the fundamental right to freedom of expression and only proceed with prosecution when a communication is more than offensive, shocking or disturbing, even if distasteful or painful to those subjected to it.

In sum, the recent changes are intended to reduce the number of prosecutions relating to social media content and to focus the prosecutions that are made to 'worthy' cases. These 'worthy' cases will involve credible threats, cases of harassment and breaches of court orders. In future, those posting offensive or shocking material that does not fit these criteria are unlikely to be prosecuted.

It remains to be seen what effect these reforms will have on the number of racially aggravated cases being brought to prosecution. Discrimination on the grounds of ethnicity or nationality has been identified as a factor which should increase the likelihood of prosecution in cases of offensive social media posts. It is now up to individual prosecutors as to how these guidelines will be interpreted. While it is unlikely that the number of racially aggravated prosecutions will increase, they may well rise as a proportion of the overall figures as the total number of prosecutions falls.

## Conclusion

Social media organisations face a difficult balancing act between providing a forum for free speech and ensuring their platforms do not become a breeding

ground for racist and other dangerous content. At the moment, these organisations are leaning too heavily towards the side of free speech. While claiming they take the problems seriously and are happy to co-operate with law
enforcement, they appear to be taking a reactive stance, doing the minimum
they can get away with in the face of public concern. Twitter, for example,
often refuses to comment on individual cases and seemingly had to be
pushed into introducing a measure such as its *report abuse* facility. Such
reluctance to take responsibility for content on its platform has earned it
much public criticism, not least from those who have been abused and threatened. While acknowledging that these organisations face some difficulties,
there are some simple measures which could be taken to help manage the
problem of racism on social media. These include streamlining their reporting facilities, being more proactive in their responses to potentially criminal
activity and being more transparent about the amount and nature of racist
content on their sites.

Similarly, the police face a number of challenges with regards to social
media. These include the sheer volume of potentially criminal content, the
anonymity of many offenders and the difficulty of compiling suitable evidence for prosecutions. The police are increasingly using social media as a
means to communicate with potential offenders and the wider public.
However, there appears to be a lack of consistency in the way that different
forces engage with social media and related offences. From the data we
obtained under the FOI, it is clear that there are big discrepancies in how different forces not only react to potential offences on social media, but also how
they record and monitor such information.

In terms of prosecuting social media offenders, the UK is currently at a
crossroads. Our figures show the number of prosecutions relating to social
media content has increased significantly in recent years, although racially
aggravated offences comprise a small proportion of these offences. New
Crown Prosecution Service guidelines look set to reduce the number of prosecutions as, in future, only content amounting to genuine threats and prolonged harassment will pass the threshold for prosecution. This reduces the
likelihood of 'heat of the moment' content being prosecuted. However,
according to the small print of the new guidelines, prosecutors should view
racially aggravated content as increasing the probability of charges being
brought. It remains to be seen what this will mean in practice.

# 4 'Race' and racisms in a digital world

## Introduction

What do we mean by 'race'? What is racism and where does it come from? Under what conditions does it thrive or whither? And what impacts has the internet had on our experience and understanding of racist behaviour? These are some of the key questions tackled in this chapter. In addressing them, it lays the foundations for discussions in later chapters exploring specific acts of racism on social media across a variety of sports.

The first section attempts to define 'race' and examine how the term has shifted in meaning over time and contexts. Section two then explores the idea of racism and the various forms it may take. Section three draws on research from other fields such as social psychology to discuss the potential causes of racist behaviour and the various conditions under which prejudice may breathe or die. Finally, section four discusses some of the ways in which ideas of 'race' and racism have been influenced by the digital world.

## 'Race'

Although the concept of 'race' has undergone much analysis, we still cannot provide a single definition of what 'race' really is. As Malik (1996: 1–2) notes, 'everyone knows what a race is but no one can quite define it'. Although Montagu (1974: 62) argues that 'race' should be dropped from vocabulary because of its unjustifiable generalisations, this would prove almost impossible as it has become entwined within elements of biology, culture, religion, politics and nation. In other words, 'race' is a 'myth that will not die' (Farrington *et al.* 2012: 153).

Ever since the European explorations of the late fifteenth century, 'race' thinking has permeated the consciousness of human groups. That said, between the sixteenth and eighteenth centuries, the term 'race' was rarely explicitly employed in the writings of clerics, historians, authors of fiction, early anthropologists and travellers (Malik 1996). However, non-white groups, and Africans in particular, were racialised as 'Other' and deemed to represent a mirror image of the civilised West or white norm (Said 1985). This mirror image not only reflected external differences, but also internal character differences. Kawash (1997: 30 in Chun 2012: 41) discusses the complexity of 'race' and how it has become a synonym for both external and internal markers.

> In this shift to a modern, biologized understanding of race, skin color becomes visible as a basis for determining the order of identities and differences and subsequently penetrates the body to become the truth of something hidden in the invisible interior of the organism (as organic or ontological). To see racial difference is therefore to see the bodily sign of race but also to see more than this seeing, to see the interior difference it stands for.

'Race' has been used as a mechanism to divide human groups on the basis of physical differences such as skin colour, facial features, cranial capacity, etc. Using skin colour as a primary marker of 'race' has been embraced by many social scientists and anthropologists, none more so than Voltaire, a French Enlightenment thinker, who claimed that 'only a blind man could doubt that the whites, Negroes, albinos, Hottentots, Laplanders, Chinese are entirely different races' (Bernasconi 2009: 90).

Yet, as Kawash (1997) notes, 'race' also refers to 'invisible' or internal characteristics such as mental capacities, endurance and temperament. Combe's (in Miles 1989: 35) observational writings during colonial times emphasise this: '[T]he Hindoo head is small, and the European large ... The Hindoo brain indicates a manifest deficiency in the organs of Combativeness and Destructiveness; while, in the European, these parts are amply developed'. This suggests that cranial capacity (external markers) results in internal character differences between 'races'. 'Race' therefore reflects a binarised view of the world as complex socio-cultural phenomena are commonly articulated in terms of good/bad, civilised/uncivilised, superior/inferior and black/white (Said 1985). These simplistic binarised representations play a crucial role in perpetuating and maintaining our racialised preoccupations.

Charles Darwin's groundbreaking work, *Origin of Species* (1859), constitutes a significant turning point in human understandings of 'race'. His theory of evolution played a major part in how we now see the world today and was hailed by many including Karl Marx, who believed that his works had broken down 'teleological conceptions of development' (Malik 1996: 90). Darwin's work was misconstrued though by Social Darwinists who argued that 'naturalised conflict between human groups ... provided both an explanation and a justification for the dominance of the strong over the weak' (Ratcliffe 2004: 18). This reified the ideology of a hierarchical structure of 'race'.

In contemporary academic literature, the idea of 'race' as a biological fact is now widely discredited by scholars and scientists. Instead, 'race' is viewed as a social construction or ideology (Miles 1989; Omi and Winant 1994) as science has never convincingly managed to separate human groups according to physical or internal characteristics. Following various UNESCO statements post-Second World War, 'race as a cultural, rather than a biological, fact seemed universally accepted, and the "two cultures" of the sciences and the humanities coalesced together around this common understanding' (Chun 2012: 41).

Despite this, the idea of 'race' has arguably become normalised and largely unquestioned in everyday life. Ratcliffe (2004: 15) refers to the tenacity of 'race' as, 'despite being devoid of scientific validity', it has 'retained a hegemonic position in public consciousness' and is used heuristically as it helps us understand the world around us. For Omi and Winant (1986), 'race' is a fundamental tenet in the organisation of social groups. They use the term 'racial formation to refer to the process by which social, economic and political forces determine the content and importance of racial categories, and by which they are in turn shaped by racial meanings' (Omi and Winant 1986: 66 in Chun 2012: 43).

'Race' therefore creates signifiers and these signifiers work to order human populations on the basis of socially constructed differences. Kawash's (1997: 130) argument on the relationship between the visible (external/signifier) and the invisible (internal/signified) is extremely poignant in this discussion.

> The modern conception of racial identity maintains an uneasy relation to the visual; the visible marks of the racialized body are only signs of deeper, interior difference, and those visible marks are the only differences that can be observed ... The modern concept of race is therefore predicated on an epistemology of visibility, but the visible becomes an insufficient guarantee of knowledge. As a result, the possibility of a gap opens up between what the body says and what the body means.

The media helps to reify and uphold our racial preoccupations as social groups, sports stars and national sports teams are often represented in narrow stereotypical contexts (Cottle 2006; Farrington *et al.* 2012; Poole and Richardson 2006; Van Dijk 1991). In a sporting context, Jamaican sprinters may signify explosive speeds while East African runners may signify endurance. Both signifiers lead to the same signified: 'natural ability'. For some, this may appear a complement and yet, for Stangor (2009: 2), 'The problem, in part, is that if we express positive stereotypes, it is assumed that we hold the negative ones, too'. For Hylton (2009: 90), 'this stereotype devalues black sporting achievement, and consoles the white athlete because they have to work harder to overcome this genetic deficiency'. As Farrington *et al.* (2012: 49) state, the natural ability stereotype appears to undermine 'intellectual capacities'.

Dyer (1997) argues that while whites remain unraced, black athletes are frequently marked by their 'raced' bodies. Non-white athletes thus become transparent as the body is used visually in the process of signification. On the other hand, whites are opaque or heterogeneous. 'Crucially, this gap between what the body says and what the body is taken to mean underlines the force of racism' (Chun 2012: 43).

## Racism(s)

Racism is a complicated term to define and understand due to its various forms and uses, and shifting nature over time. Nonetheless, Miles (1989: 149) suggests that:

> We can define racism as any set of claims or arguments which signify some aspect of the physical features of an individual or group as a sign of permanent distinctiveness and which attribute additional negative characteristics and or consequences to the individual's or group's presence.

The emphasis on physical traits that underpins racist thinking is further elaborated by Cashmore (Cashmore and Troyna 1983: 27) who notes that the consequence of this is an 'ordering' of human populations:

> Racism is the doctrine that the world's population is divisible into categories based on physical differences which can be transmitted genetically. Invariably, this leads to the conception that the categories are ordered hierarchically so that some elements of the world's population are superior to others.

Miles and Cashmore both indicate that 'race' and racism are ideologies that centre on biological difference. However, new forms of racism have emerged within contemporary society (Barker 1981; Gilroy 1992; Mason 2000; Modood 1997). For Goldberg (1990: xiii), 'the presumption of a single monolithic racism is being displaced by a mapping of the multifarious historical formulations of racisms'.

Racism is not just a passing phenomenon as it constantly develops, changes and mutates. Malcolm X (in Otis 1993: 151) once used a metaphor from popular culture to describe its shifting meaning: 'Racism is like a Cadillac. The 1960 Cadillac doesn't look like the 1921 Cadillac, but it is still a Cadillac; it has simply changed form'. This metaphor demonstrates that racism has changed from a biological to a cultural meaning within a relatively short period of time. Pilkington (2003: 18) adds that 'in the case of new racism race is coded as culture'. Whatever the detours may be, one constant remains, 'ultimately, the goal of racism is dominance' (Memmi 2009: 131). For Wetherell and Potter (in Hook 2006: 210), racism is best defined as 'the effect of establishing, sustaining and reinforcing oppressive power relations between those defined as racially or ethnically different'.

It is no longer possible to discuss racism in a singular sense. Instead we must examine racisms, in the plural. The remainder of this section will critically examine some of the most relevant and significant forms of racism.

## Overt racism

With reference to a media context, Hall (1990: 12–13) defines overt racism as: 'Those many occasions when open and favourable coverage is given to arguments, positions and spokespersons who are in the business of advancing an openly racist argument or a racist policy or view'. For example, this term could be applied to extreme right-wing groups who wish to repatriate all black or Asian communities from western countries to their country of ancestral origin or individuals and groups who actively seek out and verbally and physically abuse some minority groups. This type of racism is very visible. It could be suggested that a sensitivity now surrounds overt racism which, in turn, has led to its decrease in some social settings. For example, a recent parliamentary report concluded that racism in football is now 'significantly less common' in the UK, thanks to social changes, awareness campaigns and codes of conduct. It stated: 'The atmosphere experienced by those attending football matches has changed hugely since the 1970s and 80s when racial and other forms of abuse were common' (Culture Media and Sport Committee 2012). This is not to say that racism has gone away, rather that it has found new outlets and taken on alternative, and sometimes more subtle forms.

## Symbolic racism

While overt racism may have declined in some contexts, new and more subtle types of racism have begun to emerge and be identified. Barker (1981) has spoken of 'new racism'; others of a symbolic racism (Sears 1988), or a more subtle or aversive racism (Gaertner and Dovidio 1986). 'Symbolic racism' refers to the ethnic, religious or racial symbols that 'out-groups' display (Gilroy 1987; Van Dijk 1993). It is often based on the argument that the out-groups get more than they deserve. It is a veiled form of racism, in which it is argued that government policies for improving the position of ethnic minorities – for example by quotas – are unfair because they give collective opportunities and rights to ethnic minorities that the majority are denied. In other words contemporary racist attitudes are no longer conceptualised primarily in terms of black inferiority and segregationist sentiments, but rather in terms of abstract ideological symbols and symbolic behaviour.

Islamophobia is an example of symbolic racism, a form that affects the homogenised 'Asian' within the British context. Muslims have been presented as 'primitive, violent ... and oppressive' whereas the West is traditionally considered 'civilised, reasonable ... and non-sexist' (The Runnymede Trust 1997: 6). Following 9/11, Britain saw community relations worsen as 'anyone who wore a turban, or simply "looked Asian" was at risk of physical assault or verbal abuse' (Ratcliffe 2004: 9). In the Islamophobic era, British Muslims are stereotyped as 'dangerous social problems' (Archer 2006: 55) and stigmatised as 'terrorist warriors' (Salih 2004: 998).

Johnson (2007: 24) argues that without our noticing, Britain is 'becoming a society increasingly divided by race and religion' and as a result, British Muslims in particular are not only becoming isolated, but seen as the 'enemy within' (Allen 2007; Ratcliffe 2004). For Poole and Richardson (2006: 99), the contemporary perception of Islam is that: 'Muslim values are represented at odds with "British" values that question Muslims' ability to fit in'. Hence, British Asians appear to be on the receiving end of 'symbolic racism' within contemporary western societies (Gilroy 1987; Van Dijk 1993).

On the one hand, one could positively suggest that minority communities contribute to the cultural 'melting pot' and add a 'distinct taste to the overall group culture' (Zarate 2009: 400). On the other hand, right-wing groups promote the idea of assimilation rather than integration, thus promoting a culture that is deemed pure, unitary and fixed. Within this latter standpoint, ethnic groups are considered homogenous and incompatible with the host culture. Stereotypical perceptions of 'Others', or inferential racism, is central to this debate.

### Inferential racism

Hall (1990: 13) suggests that covert racism can be classified as inferential racism which, refers to:

> Those apparently naturalised representations of events and situations relating to 'race', whether 'factual' or 'fictional', which have racist

premises and propositions inscribed in them as a set of unquestioned assumptions. These enable racist statements to be formulated without ever bringing into awareness the racist predicates on which the statements are grounded ... Inferential racism is more widespread – and in many ways, more insidious (than overt racism), because it is largely invisible even to those who formulate the world in its terms.

In many ways inferential racism is based on 'common-sense' thinking. Problematically, stereotypes are formed without ever acknowledging the racial grounding on which they are based. Zarate (2009: 399) offers an excellent example of inferential racism as he notes

A colleague of mine ... is African American. He asks: 'How do I respond if someone tells me "You are very articulate"?' In this instance, the racism would be subtle. The person would be expressing surprise at meeting an articulate Black man. It is, however, a socially acceptable sentence and it is not explicitly racist.

In this example, racism is invisible and the colleague may be unaware that the racialisation has occurred. This type of racism is influenced by stereotypes, which Stangor (2009: 2) describes as 'the traits that come to mind quickly when we think about the groups'. Stereotypical representations of 'races', ethnicities, religions and nations can all be observed in the media, sport and wider society (Cottle 2006; Poole and Richardson 2006; Van Dijk 1991). Pervasive and persistent examples include the notion that black people are naturally better athletes, or that Asians lack the physical strength for contact sports (Farrington *et al.* 2012; Kilvington 2012). Critical Race Theory (CRT) is an approach that seeks to foreground and challenge these assumptions. Originally emerging from the field of legal studies (D.A. Bell 1980), CRT views issues of 'race' and racism as being engrained in the fabric of society, and therefore crucial to any genuine understanding of, or attempt to change, that society. Hylton (2009), among others, has applied CRT to the arena of sport and society. He has argued that the perpetuation of racial myths around sport remain a 'cancerous aspect of social life', adding: 'Society maintains the habit of reifying "race" in sport and other institutions, and a critical analysis of racism and therefore antiracism needs to challenge any "race" schema, commonsense views and other hegemonic impositions' (2008: 5).

### Institutional racism

Coates (2011a: 1) describes institutional racism as 'hidden; secret; private; covered; disguised; insidious or concealed'. While this term entered British popular discourse (Cottle 2004) with the publication of the Macpherson Report in 1999, the concept can originally be found in the writings of black activists Stokely Carmichael and Charles Hamilton. Writing in 1967 about the conditions of blacks in America, they argued that racism was not just the attitudes of a few white people but was intrinsic to US society. They note that institutional racism is harder to challenge but in many ways is more pervasive than overt racism:

> When a black family moves into a house in a white neighbourhood and is stoned, burned or routed out, they are victims of an overt act of individual racism which many people will condemn – at least in words. But it is institutional racism that keeps black people locked in dilapidated slum tenements ... The society either pretends it does not know of this latter situation.
>
> (Carmichael and Hamilton 1967: 4)

This suggests that racism, as well as being an individual act, is also a part of the fabric of society and can be seen in various settings, including the media (Price *et al.* 2013b). It can exist in the structures, policies and cultures of organisations and institutions. At times this manifestation is overt but more often it is covert and less likely to gain public condemnation or even acknowledgement (Farrington *et al.* 2012). This suggests that the foundations of contemporary racism are to be found disguised within institutions and organisations. Institutional racism is therefore very hard to identify and challenge. As Zarate (2009: 388) notes, it is possible for one to 'document the underrepresentation of minorities among elected and appointed officials', but it may be 'virtually impossible to identify any specific instance of racism'.

The pervasiveness of institutional racism is highlighted by Carmichael and Hamilton (1967: 112) who note that those with racist beliefs may 'not stone a black family', nor would they be involved in any other personal racist activity, but they may continue to support and involve themselves with institutions that perpetrate racist policies. Put simply, this form of racism 'operates as a boundary keeping mechanism whose primary purpose is to maintain social distance between racial elite and racial non-elite' (Coates 2011b: 121). Similarly, being 'colour blind' and thus ignoring that racism exists is also an example of covert racism.

### Colour blindness

Wilson and Costanza-Chock (2012: 246) postulate that the election of Barack Obama as President of the United States of America has created the illusion that we have entered a 'post-racial' era. Moreover, because overt racism towards minority groups is largely deemed 'unacceptable', there is 'a tendency to deny that discrimination is still a problem in modern U.S society' (Bodenhausen *et al.* 2009: 126). In simple terms, it is perceived that 'race' can no longer be an exclusionary force. However, denying the impact of 'race' is symptomatic of new racism.

Hylton (2009: 32) labels this denial as 'colour blindness', noting that it 'is a device that maintains dominant hegemonies and social hierarchies by regularly ignoring discriminatory factors'. For D'Andrea and Daniels (1999), acknowledging contentious issues such as 'race' and racism proves an uncomfortable experience for many white people. Thus, 'it is easier ... to avoid situations that might force them to confront the ways in which they personally benefit from the perpetuation of racism in our modern society' (D'Andrea and Daniel 1999: 98). Overlooking racism prevents it from being challenged and 'turning a blind eye' upholds white privilege and the racial status-quo.

Although having an African American in the Oval Office is without doubt a sign of progress, it fundamentally 'cannot alone erase the fact that race, class, and gender all continue to unjustly structure Americans' opportunities in every sphere of life' (Wilson and Costanza-Chock 2012: 246). As we alluded to earlier, Omi and Winant (1986) strongly argue that 'race' is a significant factor in the formation of social groups; this cannot be ignored, dismissed or denied. The multifarious affects of racism leads to the 'abuse and suffering of billions of people on Earth on a daily, hourly and secondly basis' (Farrington *et al.* 2012: 12). Although the situation has marginally improved in the last few decades, it would be incorrect to view the world in 'post-racial' terms. Racism might have changed form, but it is still as prevalent and as powerful as ever.

## The psychology of racism

In this section we look to the field of social psychology for some lessons about the causes of racism. Rather than providing an exhaustive account of this field, it summarises some of the research findings deemed most relevant to the aims and scope of this book. Why do some people behave in a racist way and others not? What are the conditions under which this behaviour is most likely? And what, if anything, can be done to reduce and tackle such behaviour?

As humans we are predisposed to categorise people (Allport 1954) and to attach general traits, or stereotypes, to these categories (Fiske and Taylor 1991). It is thought these characteristics have been developed in humans over time as they helped people make sense of their complex world and reach quick judgements in battles over scarce resources (Fiske 2010).

Lewin (1948) argued that individuals need a firm sense of group identification in order to maintain a sense of well-being. This basic idea was
developed in substantial detail in the Social Identity Theory (SIT) of Tajfel
*et al.* (Tajfel 1970, 1972, 1973, 1978, 1981). The assumption of this line of
investigation is that people employ the same cognitive processes in making
social judgements as are used in dealing with physical stimuli (Tajfel
and Wilkes 1963). Research has demonstrated that we tend to exaggerate
similarities within categories and differences between categories. With
respect to intergroup relations, the effects are that in-group members are
assumed to be similar; out-group members are seen as different (Stephan and
Stephan 1985; Wilder 1986). Wilder (1986) concludes that social categorisation is linked to a variety of cognitive processes that accentuate group differences and ethnocentrism, and thereby cause and/or escalate intergroup
conflict. One surprising aspect of the initial work on SIT by Tajfel *et al.*
(1971) was that the mere perception of belonging to a group, even an artifi-
cially created one, was sufficient to produce intergroup discrimination, that
is, in-group favouritism.

These processes may lead to prejudice. This can be defined as '...a negative evaluation of a social group or a negative evaluation of an individual
that is significantly based on the individual's group membership' (Crandall
and Eshleman 2003: 414). The prejudice experienced and/or expressed may
take a variety of forms such as 'race', gender, sexuality and social class. The
context of a situation will determine which of these categories is called upon,
along with the potential resulting stereotypes and prejudice.

Research from neuroscience suggests the above process can take place in
a fraction of a second and happens beyond our conscious selves. As Fiske
says: 'In this blink of an eye, a complex network of stereotypes, emotional
prejudices and behavioural impulses activates. These knee jerk reactions do
not require conscious bigotry, though they are worsened by it' (2010: 8). In
other words, although prejudice is not inevitable, its foundations lie in deeply
embedded behaviours. Whether or not prejudice is expressed, and the forms
it may take, depends on a number of factors. These include the social contexts in which interactions take place, the nature of the communication
taking place, the general world views and personalities of those involved,
and their particular physical and mental states at the time.

Crandall and Eshleman have described a justification-suppression model
of prejudice (2003). They argue that 'several social, cultural, cognitive, and
developmental factors create within people a variety of prejudices' (2003:
416). There is then a complex set of forces that may come into play which
either serve to justify or suppress those prejudices. 'Suppression processes
will reduce prejudice's public expression; they will also minimize its private
experience' (Crandall and Eshleman 2003: 417). Conversely, justification

processes will increase the likelihood of prejudices being expressed and may also allow individuals to justify or rationalise these expressions.

The social norms of a particular environment are thought to be important in determining whether prejudice occurs. As Stangor observes:

> People hold and express stereotypes and prejudice to the extent that they see it as appropriate, within their social contexts, to do so ... We are prejudiced because we feel that others we care about are, too – that it is ok to be so. Similarly, we are tolerant when we feel that being so is socially acceptable.
>
> (Stangor 2009: 4)

Social norms acting against prejudice exist most explicitly in the form of sanctions such as anti-racism laws. Sanctions of this kind provide external motivations against prejudice (Plant and Devine 1998). When such norms become engrained as personal values, they act as internal motivations. It could be argued that such motivations have become powerful forces checking the explicit expressions of racism in many modern contexts. For example, Bodenhausen et al. observe:

> Because there are now social penalties associated with unchecked prejudices, ranging all the way from receiving disapproving looks, to being labelled a bigot, to being fired from one's job, people develop a desire to control automatic biases to avoid the costs of nonconformity with the robust norms of egalitarianism that have come to dominate many contemporary societies.
>
> (Bodenhausen et al. 2009: 115)

However, while it could be argued that there has been a general shift in social norms against the expression of prejudice (at least in some societies), individuals have the capacity to create world-views that appear coherent with such behaviour and thereby help them to justify their actions. For example, Crandall and Eshleman (2003) have outlined a number of outlooks that are used by some people to justify prejudice, both internally and publicly. These include a belief in the value of social hierarchy, some religious attitudes towards certain groups, or the attitude that some groups are responsible for their misfortunes and therefore 'get what they deserve'. Such views may counteract wider social norms acting against expressions of prejudice.

Individual personality traits are also thought to be significant in influencing whether the processes of categorisation and stereotyping lead to expressions or actions of prejudice. Some researchers have suggested a link between racist behaviour and certain personality disorders (Billig 1978). For example, Bell (C. Bell 1980) argues that many of the characteristics often associated with racists can be found in the narcissistic personality traits identified by Kohut (1966). These include a need for attention, a lack of empathy, an inflated sense of entitlement and a response to criticism which usually involves indifference, rage or shame.

Levels of personal self-esteem are also important here. Racist attitudes and behaviour towards members of an out-group are used by some as an attempt to feel better about themselves and to win favour within their particular social group (Tajfel and Turner 1979). As Zarate notes, people are thought to desire positive self-esteem and that 'they do this by derogating relevant outgroups to make the ingroup appear more positive' (2009: 394).

Other important factors influencing the likelihood of prejudice are the nature of the communications taking place. There is evidence that anonymous communications are much more prone to expressions of prejudice (Zimbardo 1969) and often more serious forms of prejudice. In contrast, prejudice is less likely in contexts in which the actors feel they will be answerable for their actions. As Crandall and Eshleman state: 'Public, accountable behaviour shows less evidence of prejudice than private, anonymous behaviour' (2003: 421).

Similarly, face-to-face interactions are less likely to lead to discrimination than situations where communications are conducted remotely (Gaertner 1975). This may be linked to the importance of empathy as there is evidence to show that the more we know or care about someone, the less likely we are to act in a prejudicial way towards them (Stangor 2009). Related to this is the notion that prejudice is reduced when we are able to see others as individuals rather than as members of a group (Fiske 2010). Such a process though requires time and information about the person concerned, and is therefore more likely in some contexts than others.

There are also more practical determinants of prejudice linked to the conditions of the places, persons and interactions involved. For example, prejudice is more likely to be activated in an individual when they are under stress (Fiske 2010). Similarly research has shown that prejudice tends to occur when we are tired, distracted or feeling down (Stangor 2009). The very act of trying to suppress prejudicial feelings and thoughts can cause these emotions, thereby leading to a failure to successfully control one's behaviour. As Crandall and Eshleman argue: '...suppression takes mental energy, and a resultant mental fatigue can lead to suppression failures, inadvertent slips, mental backlash, and a reduced ability to self-regulate' (2003: 423). Alcohol can play a role here as research suggests it reduces our ability to inhibit and manage our actions in this context (Steele and Southwick 1985; Steele and Josephs 1990). There is also evidence to suggest that prejudice is more likely to occur when people make instant or rushed decisions. In contrast, people are more likely to refrain from prejudice when they have more time to consider their response (Bodenhausen *et al.* 2009).

So far, this section has considered the nature of prejudice and some of the conditions under which it is more or less likely to occur. Table 4.1 provides a summary of these factors and their impacts will be discussed in coming chapters in relation to use of social media across a variety of sporting contexts.

*Table 4.1* Factors affecting expressions of racism

| *Factors tending to increase expressions of racism* | *Factors tending to reduce expressions of racism* |
| --- | --- |
| *Social context* | *Social context* |
| Weak penalties/rules against prejudice on social media site | Strong penalties/rules against prejudice on social media site |
| Weak or no cultural norms against prejudice | Strong cultural norms against prejudice |
| Likely to categorise according to 'race' | Likely to categorise other than 'race' |
| World view promoting some prejudice | World view against prejudice |
| *Nature of communication* | *Nature of communication* |
| Anonymous | Identifiable |
| Invisible | Visible |
| Private (or feeling of) | Public (or feeling of) |
| Quick/instantaneous response time | Delayed response time |
| Lack of personal information about recipient(s) | Lots of personal information about recipient(s) |
| Lack of previous personal contact with recipient(s) | Lots of previous personal contact with recipient(s) |
| *Personality* | *Personality* |
| Lack of empathy | High levels of empathy |
| Low self esteem | High self esteem |
| Antisocial | Social |
| Social media is a 'game' (dissociative imagination) | Social actions have real consequences |
| *Condition* | *Condition* |
| Tired | Alert |
| Stressed | Relaxed |
| Threatened | Calm |
| Distracted | Focused |
| Drunk | Sober |

## 'Race' and racisms in the digital age

> The internet intervenes in people's daily lives across all spheres and public spaces such as public libraries, cybercafés, and school classrooms and across platforms like the cell phone, the PDA, and the television.
>
> (Nakamura 2008: 178)

As you drink your morning coffee, the presenters of your favourite breakfast programme might be interviewing the latest YouTube sensation or discussing the psychological impact of social network sites (SNS) with leading experts. In the adverts, popular internet sites may be promoted such as Netflix, Love Film or Go Compare. Instead of watching, you may decide to spend these few minutes on your Tablet or Smart Phone reading the latest status updates on Facebook, scanning last night's tweets or perusing your favourite online newspaper site, depositing a comment or two. On your commute to work, it is likely that the train/bus will be silent. Commuters are now too engrossed with their Kindle/Smart Phone or portable music device to pay any attention to their fellow passengers – being hit by broadsheet pages is on the decline. After several hours at work, your dinner hour arrives. If you are proud of your culinary delight, you may decide to upload a photo to Instagram or Flickr before tucking in. While eating, you may Google who was evicted from the latest reality show, investigate the latest football gossip or simply relax by playing Temple Run, posting your top score on one of your SNS's. Before work recommences, you may wish to tweet about an interesting article which, in turn, stimulates discussion among your digital followers. All this, and it is only midday. As Nakamura (2008) stipulates above, the internet has revolutionised how we communicate, how we interact with others, and in the process, it has become manifest in contemporary daily life experiences.

Everett (2012: 148) labels this online space 'the digital public sphere'. It has even been argued that this sphere is in fact race-neutral or even egalitarian. She notes that

> We are creating a world that all may enter without privilege or prejudice accorded by race, economic power, military force, or station of birth. We are creating a world where anyone, anywhere may express his or her beliefs, no matter how singular, without fear of being coerced into silence or conformity.
>
> (in Nakamura 2008: 181)

This utopian vision was shared by the *New Yorker* cartoon in 1993, which proclaimed that 'On the Internet nobody knows that you are a dog' (Everett 2009; Steiner 1993). This indicates that 'one's identity was so hidden on the

Web that opportunities would be widely open to all regardless of background characteristics that may have traditionally disadvantaged some people over others' (Hargittai 2012: 224). Similarly, the telecom giant MCI produced a TV commercial in the early 1990s claiming there is no 'race', no genders and no infirmities in the internet age because here 'people can communicate mind to mind'. As Everett (2012: 165) states, these examples 'were symptomatic of [America's] desire to imagine and construct colorblind or hyper-tolerant virtual communities and digital public spheres through the internet's text-driven digital environments during the late 1980s and early 1990s'. These examples present the internet as an idyllic, equal and even post-discriminatory world, one where everyone has a voice and the right to speak it.

Glaser and Kahn (2005) argue that the internet has a two-fold relationship with prejudice and discrimination. On the one hand, they agree that the internet has the potential to provide an environment for greater equality and reduced discrimination due to its capacity to hide 'social category cues'. At the same time, they predict that the nature and reach of internet use is likely to increase expressions of prejudice.

The idea that some people say and do things on the internet that they would not usually say or do in everyday life has been termed the Online Disinhibition Effect (ODE) (Suler 2004). This can take positive forms, known as benign disinhibition, such as giving larger than usual donations to a cause or charity. However, in many cases it is a negative phenomenon. This is known as toxic disinhibition and could involve either communicating or behaving *badly* toward others, or accessing content and places one would not usually visit in the offline world. Suler (2004) has described six factors which, although they interact variously with different people and contexts, generally tend to promote ODE. These factors are:

### Dissociative anonymity

This is the idea that people are able to hide some or all of their real identity when conducting activity online. By separating their online and offline identities, people are freed from the moral and psychological constraints which usually guide their behaviour. As Suler explains:

> In a process of dissociation, they don't have to own their behaviour by acknowledging it within the full context of an integrated online/offline identity. The online self becomes a compartmentalized self ... In fact, people might even convince themselves that those online behaviours 'aren't me at all'.
>
> (Suler 2004: 322)

The web is therefore potentially exciting because it gives you the opportunity to make the online you different from the offline version.

> What the web does so well is give a person the opportunity to separate the social categories we belong to, like being a female, a mother, a volleyball player, Norwegian liberal or Catholic, from the personal categories we feel, like our subjective sense of who we feel we are.
>
> (Krotoski 2013: 13)

As Turkle (1997) has argued, our identities are multiple and subjective and the internet allows us to try to make some coherence out of this. It allows us to try out new identities online, and to compartmentalise these in different online worlds.

### Invisibility

This has some overlap with anonymity but is considered an important factor on its own. Even when someone's identity is known, the fact that they cannot be seen or heard by another will increase their levels of disinhibition. If one cannot see others' physical expressions, one is less immediately aware of their dislike or distaste of our actions. When online, our eyes and ears may be blind and deaf to such rebukes, thereby encouraging disinhibition. H.G. Wells' novel, *The Invisible Man*, is fitting as the character Griffin, upon becoming invisible, alters his behaviour and starts to terrorise the population. If we apply this narrative within the ODE framework, Griffin, or social media users, turns from 'benign' to 'toxic' because when one is invisible, we become less inhibited and our behaviour changes. Such a process has also been described as 'Deindividuation' – the sense of being removed from one's identity. As Krotoski argues: 'What it means is … people feel less personally responsible for their actions and do things that are impulsive, irrational and normally restricted by their inhibitions' (2013: 111).

### Asynchronicity

This refers to the idea that online communication often has a different frequency and tempo to most offline interactions. It does not always occur in real time, with replies taking minutes, hours or days. This can lead to the feeling of not having to deal with the consequences of our actions and behaviour straight away. One is able to drop a bombshell, then turn away and worry about it another day. Again, this is a potentially disinhibiting force on people's online behaviour.

## Solipsistic introjection

This is the feeling that an online conversation is taking place within one's own mind. When one interacts online, the words of others are spoken in our heads with our own voice. The users' psychological presence has been assimilated into one's psyche. These interactions can in turn become inter-weaved with our own fantasy conversations in our head. In short, the 'online companion ... becomes a character within one's intrapsychic world, a char-acter shaped partly by how the person actually presents him or herself via text communication' (Suler 2004: 323). Again, this leads to disinhibition.

## Dissociative imagination

The creation of imaginary, online characters encourages some to believe they are taking part in a separate world, apart from the usual constraints of real life. People may develop the belief that once the computer is turned off, they can rejoin their everyday life and are not responsible for what happened in that other world. Because of dissociative imagination, then, some social media users speak more freely and openly as they feel that their online being is operating in a 'make-believe dimension' (Suler 2004: 323).

## Minimisation of status and authority

Many of the visible signals of status and authority do not feature in the online world and so there is some sense of a level playing field in which all can have a say. When these visible cues are removed, people may become disinhibited. As Suler describes: 'A fear of disapproval and punishment from on high dampens the spirit. But online, in what feels more like a peer rela-tionship – with the appearances of authority minimized – people are much more willing to speak out and misbehave' (2004: 324).

The above factors are deemed significant in promoting ODE and therefore have the potential to promote racist behaviour. They are not the only important factors, but they interact with other social and psychological factors (such as those described in the section above) to produce various effects across different contexts.

As Suler (2004) would suggest then, the internet provides a 'backstage' environment in which users feel free to express racist opinions and material. Hylton argues: 'Through the seeming privacy of the Internet, its individual-istic communications process and the relative anonymity of the interactants, cyberspace becomes a "safe space" for normally borderline and more abhor-rent views' (2013: 14). That said, it could be argued that anonymity is becoming increasingly difficult in recent times. This is due to a trend towards authenticity on social media sites, cultural shifts in what is considered personal or private information, and the actions of some online users to reveal the identities of others. However, if this is the case, what remains a powerful force is the feeling of privacy that the internet can provide its users. Although most, if not all, internet activity leaves a trace, some users believe that their cyber-beings are protected and thus they feel hidden. This perception of privacy may encourage expressions of prejudice (Glaser and Kahn 2005).

Also relevant here are the potential speeds of communication and response provided by the internet. The immediate nature of many interactions does not always lend itself naturally to restrained and considered commentary. When this is combined with a perception of privacy and anonymity, the context may be one in which many of the social barriers to expressions of prejudice are removed. In other words, then, online communities' instantaneous access to social media platforms, feelings of privacy, and the informal nature of most web posts can all lead users to post racist reactions to real world events without a second of hesitation.

If the nature of internet use appears significant in shaping communications about 'race', then issues of 'race' also appear important in how the internet is used. In other words, issues of 'race' shape our online experiences (Boyd 2011; Everett 2012; Hargittai 2012; Nakamura 2008). For Boyd (2011), our SNS preferences have been influenced by issues of 'race', ethnicity and socio-economics, i.e. the categories that help construct social structures. Boyd (2011: 203) researched how 'race' and class shaped American teen engagement with MySpace and Facebook, suggesting that 'teens choose to self-segregate across the two sites, just as they do in schools'. It was noted that white American teens tended to migrate from MySpace to Facebook because of issues relating to features and functionality, values and goals, notions of class, uploaded content, perceptions of safety but most importantly, because of friend networks. Boyd (2011: 218), who labels this migration 'digital white flight', attempts to draw parallels between the offline and online worlds:

> The first teens to move to the 'suburbs' were those who bought into a Teen Dream of collegiate maturity, namely those who were expressly headed towards dorm-based universities and colleges. They were the elite who were given land in the new suburbs before plots were broadly available. The suburbs of Facebook signalled more mature living, complete with digital fences to keep out strangers. The narrative that these digital suburbs were safer than the city enhanced its desirability, particularly for those who had no interest in interacting with people who were

different. Some teens were moved because of the policies of their parents. Early settlers incentivized their friends to join them.

(ibid.)

White teens migrated from the 'ghetto' of MySpace, and settled in the prestigious, affluent and safer suburb of Facebook, along with their white friends. This contrasts with recent figures from the United States suggesting that Twitter has high usage among young African Americans. Of 18–29 year old African Americans who use the internet, 40 per cent say that they use Twitter. This is 12 percentage points higher than the comparable figure for young whites (Smith 2014).

This recent research suggests a digital divide persists among different demographic groups. White Americans are more likely to use the internet than black Americans, but the differences are most pronounced when age and levels of education are taken into account. For example, just 45 per cent of black seniors are internet users, and 30 per cent have broadband at home, compared to white seniors of whom 63 per cent go online and 51 per cent are broadband adopters (Smith 2014). Nakamura (2008) argues that 'more connected' groups posses a 'digital advantage'. In short, because some groups are less connected, they miss out on many of the opportunities and benefits that the internet can provide. The inequalities of the offline world are therefore reflected and reinforced by those of the online world.

## Conclusion

Although 'race' may be a myth, in the sense of having no clear biological foundation, it is a living, breathing concept affecting the lives and interactions of many people. It certainly exists in the racisms that many people have to endure on a daily basis.

'Race' is one of the categories people may reach to in order to make sense of their world. We are, by nature, categorisers. This happens in fractions of seconds and often beyond our awareness. Much of the time it is a useful process allowing us to simplify and understand the complexities around us. But at other times it lays the foundations for prejudice and discrimination.

This chapter has discussed some of the key factors affecting how and where prejudice may be expressed (see Table 4.1). These factors include wider social contexts such as laws and cultural norms; personality traits such as levels of empathy and self esteem; communication factors such as anonymity, privacy and prior experience and knowledge of recipients; and physical conditions such as stress, tiredness and drunkenness. The chapter has also discussed some of the characteristics of internet use which may lead to disinhibition and affect expressions of racism. These include feelings of anonymity and privacy, and the capacity to create and dissociate online and offline identities.

Some have argued that the internet could bring about the achievement of an electronic global village (Negroponte 1995) in which differences would not matter – a 'post race' space. In this view, the social problems and negative connotations that often go together with physical indicators of difference would potentially also disappear. However, this is far from the case. In fact, there is evidence to suggest that the 'Internet can and does enable new and insidious forms of racism' (Nakamura 2002: 30).

Though visual signifiers of 'race' may be absent online, recent research suggests that 'race' takes on a linguistic form (Glaser *et al.* 2002; Kang 2000; Nakamura 2002). Racial and social divides that exist offline are, in some cases, even more apparent in the digital media space (Everett 2008). Van Dijk (2005: 7) warns that 'deepening divides are byproducts of old inequalities, digital technology is intensifying inequalities, and new inequalities are appearing'.

It is therefore important, we argue, to consider internet and social media content from the same critical perspective from which we should examine offline content. The attitudes and ideologies about 'race' found offline are often reproduced and disseminated in social media and online. The internet is rooted in our physical 'real' world and is heavily influenced by the culture and ideologies of this world. As Kolko *et al.* (2000: 4–5) explain:

> Race matters in cyberspace precisely because all of us who spend time online are already shaped by the ways in which race matters off-line, and we can't help but bring our own knowledge, experiences, and values with us when we log on.

In subsequent chapters this book seeks to critically explore these issues, and what can best be done to address them, in one particular aspect of the online world – that of social media.

# 5  Football, racism and social media

## Introduction

Social media has been a mixed blessing for the world of football, offering players on the one hand an opportunity to engage with fans and promote their personal brand, but, on the other, to regularly put their foot in it (Price *et al.* 2012). For example, former Liverpool player Ryan Babel was censured by the Football Association after re-tweeting a mocked-up picture of referee Howard Webb in a Manchester United shirt immediately following his handling of a match between the two clubs. In another incident, Aldershot Town striker Marvin Morgan was put up for transfer after posting 'I hope you all die' in response to being jeered by the Football League Two side's own supporters. Meanwhile, Manchester United's Wayne Rooney got involved in a heated exchange with the fan of a rival club which resulted in the England international tweeting: 'I'll put you asleep within 10 seconds hope u turn up if u don't gonna tell everyone ur [sic] scared u little nit. I'll be waiting'.

This chapter will explore the ambivalent relationship between football and social media in the context of racism. It begins by examining the problem of footballers receiving racist abuse on social media, looking first at a high profile case in which the offender was jailed, before analysing a series of other incidents. These sections will analyse the potential causes of such cases and discuss some of the public reaction to them. This is followed by a discussion of incidents in which footballers themselves have got into trouble for publishing 'race' related content on social media, before a final section analysing how the football authorities are dealing with these issues.

## Social media racist abuse of footballers: the case of Liam Stacey

In March 2012, Bolton Wanderers footballer Fabrice Muamba collapsed during a match and lay on the pitch receiving treatment for a suspected heart attack. Many watching thought the player was dead or about to die. Meanwhile, a 21-year-old university student was out drinking with friends, watching a televised rugby international. On hearing the news of Muamba's collapse, the student tweeted his thoughts on the incident – just days later he would make international headlines for being sent to prison for his social media outburst.

Liam Stacey, of Pontypridd, South Wales, had tweeted:

LOL. F*ck Muamba. He's dead!!! #haha.

The biology student then received a number of abusive messages in response to his comments. He in turn replied with a string of racist tweets:

... go suck muamba's dead black dick then you aids ridden twat #muamasdead

.. .owwww go suck a nigger dick you fucking aids ridden cunt

... you are a silly cunt ... Your mothers a wog and your dad is a rapist. Bonjour you scruffy northern cunt

Stacey's comments were passed on to the police by a number of other Twitter users and he began to realise he may be in trouble. At first he tried to pass it off as a joke gone wrong, tweeting:

... only taking the piss. Obviously people can't take a joke.

Then he apologised and started to claim that his account had been hacked – a commonly used excuse by those accused of racism on Twitter:

I am awfully apologetic about anything I have said. I do not condone anything that has been said! My account has been hacked...

He also employed another common tactic of those accused of racism, that of denying they are a racist:

I am not a racist and I am not a person that will ever discriminate against others. This is a huge misunderstanding.

The day after his abusive tweets, Stacey was charged under the Racially Aggravated s4A Public order Act 1986. At the subsequent court hearing he pleaded guilty to the offence and was ordered to serve 56 days in prison, eventually serving half of that sentence. Passing sentence, District Judge John Charles told Stacey:

> It was racist abuse via a social networking site instigated as a result of a vile and abhorrent comment about a young footballer who was fighting for his life. At that moment, not just the footballer's family, not just the footballing world but the whole world were literally praying for his life. Your comments aggravated this situation. I have no choice but to impose an immediate custodial sentence to reflect the public outrage at what you have done.
>
> (Morris 27 March 2012)

The decision to imprison Stacey for his tweets divided opinion and provoked responses from many including legal experts, journalists, campaign groups and celebrities. On the one hand, some thought it a fair punishment and one that would help deter others from making similar comments online. For example, Lord Alan Sugar responded with a tweet saying:

> …BLOODY GOOD JOB. Be warned idiots!

Richard Madeley, in a comment piece for the *Express*, wrote:

> Fifty-six days in the slammer for that and not one too few … So-called 'trolls' – the perverts, bullies and racists who abuse others on social networking sites – need to know that they can be tracked down.
>
> (Express Online 31 March 2012)

The notion that the prison sentence given to Liam Stacey might act as a deterrent to other potential offenders was a commonly expressed idea. It was certainly evident in the thinking of the Crown Prosecution Service at the time of the case. Jim Brisbane, Chief Crown Prosecutor for the Crown Prosecution Service (CPS) Cymru-Wales, said: 'Racist language is inappropriate in any setting and through any media. We hope this case will serve as a warning to anyone who may think that comments made online are somehow beyond the law.'

These sentiments have been echoed by Clarke Carlisle, footballer and former Chairmen of the Professional Footballers Association, who said:

> Offenders should be prosecuted if the law is broken. That is simple. Swift, efficient and strict governance is the best way to tackle the problem. When people see and feel the repercussions of such actions, then they are deterred from indulging in them.
>
> (Interview 4 September 2013)

There was, however, also widespread criticism of the decision to jail Stacey. Many observers felt it was an overreaction while others claimed Stacey had been unfairly dealt with because he had targeted someone in the public limelight.

For example, Thomas Hammarberg, the council of Europe's commissioner for human rights, said:

> It [Liam Stacey's sentence] was too much. He shouldn't have gone to prison. To put him in prison was wrong ... People are at a loss to know how to apply rules for the traditional media to the new media. It's tricky and that's why there needs to be a more thorough discussion about this.
>
> (Bowcott April 2012)

The sentence also provoked much criticism from commentators in the media. Interestingly, this criticism could be found in publications from both the left and right of the political spectrum.

Joan Smith, writing for the *Independent*, said:

> A custodial sentence is wildly excessive and has worrying implications for freedom of expression, which is too important a subject to be brushed aside on grounds of 'public outrage' ... What we can do is challenge such people without engaging at the same level – trolls thrive on the adrenalin rush of invective – while trying to work out what fuels outpourings of abuse. In Stacey's case that could have been achieved through a community sentence, combined with the realisation that he has to live with the shame of his actions.
>
> (Smith 1 April 2012)

Abhijit Pandya, writing for Mail Online, similarly expressed the idea that the courts had got it wrong on this occasion. This piece directly challenged the logic of the sentencing judge (see above), arguing that the emotional and public nature of the case meant the court needed to be extra careful to be dispassionate in its outcome. It said:

> Law is about dispassion, diligence, about delivering a measured response. It is about controlling public anger for vengeance through tempered reason, particularly when the desire for a particular result may have caught the public mood. So when Stacey's object of attack was Fabrice Muamba, rightfully a figure of public sentiment and compassion, the legal system had to be extra-careful to ensure the circumstances did not override its judgment. It failed.
>
> (Pandya 28 March 2012)

The decision to send Stacey to prison also provoked strong and contrasting opinions from the wider public. For example, the *Sun*'s online story (2013) about the jail sentence inspired 315 reader comments. Of those expressing a view about the sentence, 80 supported the decision to jail Stacey while 95 were opposed. Comments in favour of the sentence fell broadly into two camps. First, there were those that felt that Stacey's Twitter rant was so bad that a custodial sentence was fully deserved. For example:

> Racism in this day and age should not be tolerated, and no thought was spared for his poor family or team mates, drink is no excuse, and words do more damage then anyting else, good on the justice system for once!!!

Other comments took a longer term view and backed the jail sentence in the hope that it would act as a deterrent against online racism. For example:

> I think they should be hard on him to set an example to these sad people who sit behind computers bullying people!! Hopefully some of these trolls are shaking in their boots now and maybe might think twice before they say cruel words on the internet.

Comments critical of the sentence came from a more diverse set of viewpoints. One of the most common criticisms was that the ruling was an affront to the concept of free speech. In this view, the case was a further step towards a 'Big Brother' society or 'police state'. Many of these comments began with a caveat about the awful nature of Stacey's comments before, in some form or another, defending his right to make them. For example:

> Its definitely not OK to say those things, but I am worried about freedom of speech, the man is an idiot, but in a democracy you have thousands of opinions and we have the right to be offended if we want but then say it or twitter it right back.

These types of opinions provoked some discussion within the trail of comments about the nature of free speech in relation to racist abuse and about language likely to incite racial hatred. For example:

> In 1998, the United Kingdom incorporated the European Convention, and the guarantee of freedom of expression it contains in Article 10, into its domestic law under the Human Rights Act. However there is a broad sweep of exceptions including threatening, abusive, and recently and controversially insulting speech or behavior likely to cause a breach of

the peace (which has been used to prohibit racist speech targeted at individuals), so that takes care of the 'it was freedom of speech' argument.

Others attacked the sentence on slightly different grounds, claiming that the 'harsh' punishment was due to the fact that Muamba was a famous footballer and his case had been in the public spotlight. In this view, the judge in the case had been influenced by high profile nature of the case and would not have handed out the same sentence if the victim at the heart of the incident had been previously unknown. In fact, many comments suggested such a case would not have even come to court. For example:

> This is ridiculous. It was because he is a celebrity. I have had a troll on my case for over a year … But the police have done nothing. Told me to ignore him. It is just plain wrong to treat a case differently because a person is in the public eye.

Other comments compared the sentence to recent cases, arguing that justice was not being applied equally or fairly. Some referred to their own experiences, as in the following extract:

> This appears to be a man who said some really nasty and unforgivable things. He has been sent to prison for 2 months, The man who burgled my home got community service, even though he had 23 convictions including burglary, assault, robbery & drugs.

Further comments brought 'race' directly into the discussion, suggesting that Stacey had been unfairly treated because he was a white man. These comments referred, often vaguely, to other cases in which the perpetrators were perceived as having got off lightly in comparison:

> yet the poppy burners got a £50 fine, he deserved to go to prison don't get me wrong but the poppy burning and the homecoming protests were a much bigger disgrace and those responsible got a slap on the wrist. It seems to me that in the UK if your white and say or do some thing bad against an ethnic minority your finished but if your from an ethnic minority you can say and do any thing you want against a white person and nothing will happen.

Stacey himself later reflected on his Twitter outburst in a BBC interview following his release from prison. He said he had drunk a lot on the day of the incident, had not intended on being a racist but had not been in the 'right frame of mind'. He apologised and expressed remorse for his comments.

When asked to try to explain his actions, he said: 'It was drunken stupidity – that's the only thing I can say about it. I don't know why I did it. I really don't' (BBC Online 22 May 2012).

For now, the last word on the case can be left to Fabrice Muamba himself, who says that, while mystified by Stacey's actions, he holds no grudges against the young man:

> I have never met him [Stacey]. I have no control over what's happened. All I can say is I hope he has learned his lesson and he doesn't go back to his old ways and moves on because I don't hold any grudges. At the end of the day, you know, he did what he did – what he had to do. I don't know what motivation was behind it, but he got punished for it. Right, now let's just move on ... I would meet him. I've got no problem against the guy. I would say 'listen, you have just got to be careful, right. Because at the end of the day there are people who are a lot worse than me who will come after you in a very different way ... It's easy to pick someone who will just, like, smile than to pick somebody who you don't know what he is capable to do'.
>
> (Interview 15 November 2013)

## Social media racist abuse of footballers: other cases

Early in 2014, Michael Convery, 43, of Linthouse, Glasgow, was also jailed for six months for racially abusing two Rangers footballers on Twitter. Convery targeted players Maurice Edu and Kyle Bartley after a game against St Johnstone in January 2012, using monkey related insults and referring to Bartley as a 'dead coon walking'. Glasgow Sheriff Court heard the players had been shocked and intimidated by the abuse before re-tweeting the comments to publicly highlight the problem. During his prosecution Convery came up with various explanations for what had happened, claiming his account had been hacked, blaming his 16-year-old son and saying he had been suffering from food poisoning on the day of the offences and drifting in and out of sleep (Daily Record 2014).

While Stacey and Convery have made the headlines for being sent to prison for their offensive tweets, there have been a number of similar cases which have received less severe punishments. In June 2011, a Norwich fan became the first to be banned for life by a football club following a racist tweet aimed at new signing James Vaughan. Luke O'Donoughoe, then a 23-year-old, from Johnson Place, was charged under the Communications Act 2003, pleaded guilty, and was sentenced to a 12-month community order and 120 hours of unpaid work. The incident was brought to light partly through the involvement of BBC pundit and former footballer Mark Bright who explained:

When James Vaughan joined Norwich from Everton, I tweeted to say, 'Good luck to James Vaughan with his move to Norwich'. Someone replied to say, 'I don't want any more blacks at Norwich. We've got enough, if you want to watch blacks and foreigners, go to see Arsenal'. I retweeted what he'd written and, to the enormous credit of Norwich fans, they hammered the guy, the club banned him for life and he ended up in the national papers.

(Dirs 17 November 2011)

In another case in early 2012, Joshua Cryer, a 21-year-old Newcastle University law student, was prosecuted after sending a series of racist tweets to broadcaster, and former footballer, Stan Collymore.

One message, sent from user @joshuacryer1, read:

Has anyone ever called you Stan Cooneymore.

Another said:

Has anyone ever referred to you as semi pro as in a semi pro coon.

Collymore re-tweeted the messages to his then 170,000 followers before sending a message back:

Not having this crap anymore. Joshua, I see you've deleted your tweets. I haven't.

Following a complaint from Collymore to the police, Cryer was charged and convicted under section 127 of the Communications Act 2003 and sentenced to a two-year community order (240 hours work). Passing sentence, District Judge Stephen Earl told Cryer he had been 'foolish, immature and pathetic' but that he thought a prison sentence would serve no useful purpose. He said:

I don't doubt you are not an inherently racist person, but you did act in an intentionally racist way. You intended to get a rise out of Mr Collymore. He has made a justifiable and reasoned stance against you to the point where you shut down your Twitter account. I find it difficult to fathom what on Earth you thought you were doing. It was stupid, and you ought to have known better. You were a legend in your own head in this attention-seeking moment.

(Wainwright 21 March 2012)

In February, 2012, Sunderland fan Peter Copeland, 29, of West Rainton, County Durham, was convicted of two counts under the Malicious Communications Act. He pleaded guilty, was given a suspended four month prison sentence and ordered to do 150 hours community service. Copeland had tweeted a comment about the Newcastle star striker Demba Ba's lips exploding. In another, also directed at a Newcastle United fan, he said:

> With the number of darkies in your fucking team, you should be called the Coon Army.

He was arrested after a journalist, working for the Newcastle Evening Chronicle and Journal titles, reported the tweets to Northumbria police.

Also in Newcastle, in February 2012, two 17-year-olds were given police warnings for sending racist tweets to Newcastle United footballer Sammy Ameobi. The decision not to prosecute the youths was taken by the CPS after consulting with the football club involved and the player himself. Following the incident, Wendy Williams, district crown prosecutor at CPS North East, said: 'Our policy is to prosecute racist and religious crime fairly, firmly and robustly. In deciding what constitutes "fairness" for such cases, the views of the victim themselves are incredibly important' (*Guardian* 7 February 2012).

In July 2013, labourer Ben Townsend was sentenced to 200 hours of community service and ordered to pay £500 compensation to two footballers he had abused on Twitter. The 25-year-old, from Cheltenham, targeted the Northampton Town players Adebayo Akinfenwa and Clarke Carlisle after their side defeated Cheltenham Town in the semi-final of League Two Play Offs. The tweets used language such as 'monkey boy' and 'coon'. Townsend pleaded guilty to two charges under the Malicious Communications Act. He had been arrested and charged after Clark Carlisle, the then Chairman of the Professional Footballers Association, reported him to police. During his court hearing, Townsend's lawyer said that he had had a 'few drinks' and been 'frustrated' by the match result when he posted the messages on Twitter.

There have been other cases in which the police have taken to Twitter themselves in order to warn and confront those posting racist abuse on social media. For example, England internationals Ashley Young and Ashley Cole were the target of such abuse by a number of Twitter users after they missed penalties during England's defeat to Italy in Euro 2012. One of the abusers called himself Steve and used the Twitter username @Lapwnage. Among his messages he tweeted:

> both Ashley Young and Ashley Cole missed penalties, another reason why niggers/monkeys shouldn't take PKs

When the tweeter was confronted by other Twitter users and threatened with police action he responded:

> All I got to say is this was just a joke, you guys need to relax, police know I was kiddin around and they won't bother me hopefully, cheers

However, the police used Twitter to challenge this notion. West Midlands police's Twitter account replied with:

> Wrong. Your comments may constitute a public order offence. We have advised complainants how to officially report this to police

The police force responded directly to other trolls and posted a message informing other users how to report racist abuse they spotted on Twitter. A number of the accounts from which the racist abuse was posted were swiftly removed by their creators. However, the police issued the following warning:

> We are well aware of this but every online interaction leaves a trace which specialist investigators can identify.

Twitter is not the only social media platform on which footballers are open to abuse. Former Gillingham striker Mark McCammon had a racist death threat posted on his Facebook page in June 2013. The Barbadian had previously received £68,000 in damages after winning an employment tribunal in which he claimed unfair dismissal by Gillingham on the grounds of racial victimisation. McCammon felt that he and other black players at the club were treated differently from their white colleagues.

The Facebook post read:

> You fucking black cunt!!! NEVER come anywhere near Gillingham again or you will get your nigger throat cut!!!

The matter was reported to the police but McCammon was critical of their response. He took matters into his own hands by putting a link to the comment on his Twitter feed asking people to help locate and identify the sender. Following a number of responses a man was arrested and bailed. McCammon said:

> They [footballers] shouldn't tolerate it, they should adopt zero tolerance and we are nowhere near zero tolerance in the game at the moment. We need to report it immediately; we need to report it to the police and ensure justice is carried out.

(Kick It Out 12 July 2013)

Bolton and England-under-21 striker Marvin Sordell also received threats on Facebook. A mocked up image of the footballer being shot was posted on the site with the message 'Don't fuck with the Millwall'. Sordell had previously claimed that he and some of his Bolton teammates had received racist abuse when playing at Millwall's New Den ground. Shortly afterwards, in 2013, his manager Dougie Freedman revealed that the player was becoming 'obsessed' with using Twitter and Facebook. The club responded by removing the striker's phone. Freedman said: 'It could be bordering on an obsession with Twitter and Facebook and all the things that go on with these kids. We are now trying to work with Marvin – by taking his phone off him' (Byrne 2013).

The above cases are the ones that have come to public attention through the media because they resulted in police or criminal action being taken. But these cases are the exceptions. Many incidents of abuse receive no official response or sanction. It is estimated that more than 500 professional footballers in the English game have a Twitter feed (Price *et al.* 2013a). This leaves them all potentially open to abuse of various kinds – including racism. As Roisin Wood, director of Kick It Out, says: 'We have incidents every weekend of this type of abuse. In my view it's a problem that is only going to get worse as social media is not going to go away' (Interview 8 March 2013). Bobby Barnes, deputy chairman of the Professional Footballers' Association (PFA), said:

> Twitter in particular presents footballers, and especially young footballers, with a problem as you get clowns on there saying things they would never say in person. There is something about being able to hide behind a computer screen which encourages this kind of behaviour.
>
> (Interview 14 March 2013)

There is certainly relevance in Barnes' suggestion that social media encourages some people to behave in ways that they would not usually consider acceptable. Roisin Wood, director of Kick It Out, believes:

> The problem on social media is a combination of anonymity and escalation. People feel anonymous on social media and think they can get away with this stuff. And if you look it often seems to begin with quite low level stuff but then gets worse and worse as they encourage each other and the whole thing escalates.
>
> (Interview 8 March 2013)

Clarke Carlisle, the former chairman of the PFA, supports this view, saying: 'There is a train of thought that social media is faceless and the user isn't accountable for what they publish, therefore there is an element of impunity about how it is used' (Interview 4 September 2013). These comments lend support to the concept of 'backstage' racism (Feagin 2010). This is the idea that the internet, and social media, provides some with a *seemingly* safe and hidden space for racism to be expressed.

However, the above cases suggest that what is happening is caused by more complex factors than straight forward anonymity. The cases discussed above are examples of some of those which have reached the courts and so, by definition, the offenders have been able to be identified by police. There are many other cases in which the offenders will not have been able to be identified. However, what the above cases show is that in at least some incidents of online abuse, offenders make no real effort to hide their real identity. Liam Stacey, for example, had the Twitter username @liamstacey9. Similarly, Joshua Cryer had the username @joshuacryer1. A more plausible explanation perhaps lies in the factors identified as producing the Online Disinhibition Effect (Suler 2004). As discussed in Chapter 4, these suggest that online users have the capacity to separate and compartmentalise their online and offline selves, thereby freeing them from the moral constraints which usually guide their behaviour. So, even when people have not fully hidden their 'real' identities on social media, they still dissociate themselves from these identities while active online. This process is further encouraged by other contributing factors including a feeling of invisibility, a lack of eye contact and other physical cues, and the asynchronicity of responses (Suler 2004). These factors are given extra plausibility by the attempted explanations of some of the offenders. Liam Stacey, for example, talked of being unable to properly explain the actions of his online self and said he had been in a different 'frame of mind'.

A recurring factor in many cases is the influence of alcohol. Stacey said he was very drunk when he sent his offensive tweets and the explanation of drunkenness was similarly used in mitigation by the solicitors defending a number of the above offenders. As discussed in Chapter 3, there is evidence to suggest the consumption of alcohol has the potential to reduce one's capacity to suppress expressions of prejudice (Steele and Southwick 1985; Steele and Josephs 1990). It is too simplistic to say Stacey was racist because he was drunk. However, that he was drunk may have contributed to the fact that he was so publicly racist on this particular occasion. In the often boozy world of football, there is evidence here to suggest that drink is often an important factor in outbursts of online racist abuse.

Some have argued that openly and directly challenging expressions of racism may have a positive impact (Zarate 2009). The above cases provide mixed support for this argument. The lessons of the Stacey case, for example, are that, in the immediate term, such challenges seemed to provoke him into further and ever more explicit expressions of racism. However, once he realised that the situation had escalated and that the authorities might become involved, he began to backtrack. Furthermore, in the longer term, there is evidence to suggest that the consequences of his actions have left him sincerely remorseful and contrite. The issue of whether or not these consequences were justified have provoked considerable debate, as discussed above.

There is also mixed evidence for the idea that prejudice is more likely to occur when people make impulsive or rushed decisions (Bodenhausen *et al.* 2009). In some of the above cases, this is clearly true. Stacey, for example, was responding quickly to a barrage of replies to his initial, provocative message. Similarly, Peter Copeland was engaged in quick fire banter with a rival supporter, while Ben Townsend was reacting to a frustrating match result. Fiske (2010) and Rowe (2004) have identified such outbursts as knee-jerk reactions to dramatic events, which can in turn lead to 'heat of the moment' defences (Long and Hylton 2002). In contrast though, Joshua Cryer sent at least seven messages over a number of days in what the prosecution described as a deliberate and considered attempt to get a reaction from Stan Collymore. In other words, we have evidence of two different forms of racist abuse: the impulsive, quick-fire abuse hurled in response to a comment or result, and the more premeditated, slow-burning abuse which seeks to get a reaction from its victim. Social media clearly provides the apparatus required for both of these forms of racism.

What these different forms of abuse have in common is the desire to play for and provoke an audience. Here we have social media as performance, with the whole world its stage. It is upon this stage that many footballers themselves seek to perform. How they do this will be the subject of the following section.

## Footballers' misuse of social media

While the above section examined cases of footballers receiving abuse on social media, this section will look at incidents where players have landed themselves in trouble for 'race' related comments on social media. In one of the most extreme cases, semi-professional footballer Shaun Tuck was jailed for 12 weeks after publishing a series of threatening, racist tweets following the killing of soldier Lee Rigby in May 2013. The 26-year-old Witton Albion striker was drunk at the time. Among his tweets included the messages:

All the mosques in England should be gassed or bombed, or stormed by 50 lads with machetes, swords the lot. And make a statement...

Am raging in me loft here yno ... Got the balaclava out, dusted down an ready for the meet. I'd be going through there door mate an taking there kids head off an killing whoever was in site!!

Go f\*\*king nuts!!! About time this country fought back. EDL are in Woolwich now!! What I'd give to be there with them now #flop #flop #flop #curryheadseverywhere

Appearing at Liverpool Magistrates Court, Tuck, of Mollington Avenue, Norris Green, pleaded guilty to a charge under the Communications Act. Sentencing him, District Judge Miriam Shelvey said he had tweeted at a time of 'heightened racial tension' and that 'these tweets contained threats of violence to innocent persons, including children, who would be victims solely because of their religion. They were promoting hatred of other community members entirely because of their religious beliefs' (Kick It Out 10 July 2013). Tuck's defence lawyer denied he was a racist.

In July 2012 Swiss footballer Michel Morganella was expelled from his side's Olympic squad for a tweet sent after Switzerland were beaten 2–1 by South Korea. The 23-year-old posted that South Koreans 'can go burn' and referred to them as a 'bunch of mongoloids'. Following his expulsion, Morganella said: 'I made a huge mistake after a disappointing result ... I wish to apologise to the people in South Korea and their team, but also to the Swiss delegation and Swiss football in general'. Swiss coach Gian Gilli said: 'He discriminated, insulted and violated the dignity of the South Korean football team and people' (BBC Online 30 July 2012).

West Ham striker Carlton Cole has experienced problems on Twitter both as a receiver and sender of information. Cole was the target of an abusive, racist post following his side's defeat to Swansea in August 2012. He responded by tweeting:

Listen, i take racism a lot lighter than others and i do understand the banter that comes a long with it to get under peoples skin but... it can sometimes be hurtful & insulting, i don't mind when people criticise me for having a bad game or they think I'm crap at football... but just say that, whether i am crap or had a bad game has nothing to do with my race, creed or religion. lets just keep it FOOTBALL. Kapeesh?

However, Cole himself had previously been charged with bringing the game into disrepute and fined £20,000 by the Football Association (FA) for posting messages about Ghanaian fans during their side's friendly with England in 2011. His tweets said:

Immigration has surrounded the Wembley premises! I knew it was a trap!

The only way to get out safely is to wear an England jersey and paint your face w/the St George's flag!

Cole later apologised for any offence caused by his comments and said that they had been intended as a light-hearted joke.

Back in 2008 winger Sam Deering was fined by his then club, Oxford United, for posting a racist message on his Facebook page. He had been in hospital recovering from an operation when he changed his Facebook status to: 'Sam is not very amused in this hospital bed, so bored!'. A friend replied with the message: 'Hope you have got some sexy nurses looking after you'. To which Deering responded: 'Nah there [sic] fucking pakis LOL'. Although made during an online conversation, the comments could be viewed by more than 1,000 of his Facebook friends. Oxford Chairman Kelvin Thomas said: 'Knowing Sam and his background I am confident that he is not a racist, however he must understand that he is a role model and even his throwaway comments have an impact on people's lives' (Mail Online 31 December 2008).

But perhaps the most high profile case of a footballer landing themselves in trouble for a racially related message involved Manchester United's Rio Ferdinand. In August 2012 the defender was fined £45,000 for improper conduct by the FA after endorsing a tweet about Chelsea's Ashley Cole which made reference to his 'race'.

Ferdinand had received a Twitter message saying:

Looks like Ashley Cole's going to be their choc ice. Then again he's always been a sell out. Shame on him.

The former England defender responded with:

I hear you fella! Choc ice is classic! hahahahahahha!!

The tweets followed Cole's court appearance as a defence witness for team-mate John Terry in which Terry was subsequently cleared of racially abusing Rio Ferdinand's brother Anton in a Premier League match. The term 'choc ice' was a reference to Cole's part in this. As former NBA basketball player John Amaechi explains, the term is sometimes used as an insult to suggest someone is black only in skin colour rather than behaviour. Amaechi says:

It's a highly derogatory term. It's a dangerous term because it allows black boys especially but black people in general, to believe that there is a way of being black that is somehow distinct from being white … It's a deeply offensive term with racial connotations.

(BBC Online 17 August 2012)

In passing judgement on Rio, the FA's commission stated it accepted that Ferdinand was not a racist but that his tweet had been abusive and insulting and made reference to Cole's 'ethnic origin, colour or race'. This was deemed an aggravating factor and increased the punishment. Following the conclusion of the FA hearing, a statement released on behalf of Ashley Cole said: 'Ashley appreciates that tweeting is so quick it often results in offhand and stray comments' (BBC Online 17 August 2012).

The above cases are examples of how social media, and Twitter in particular, exposes footballers in a number of ways. It exposes them in the positive sense of breaking down barriers with fans and by reducing the tight grip of club PR machines on the game's public profile (Price *et al.* 2013a). However, it exposes them to potential abuse (as discussed in the section above) and to potentially costly misjudgements and mistakes in their own published posts (discussed in this section). So how are the footballing authorities responding to these issues? And what help and advice is available to footballers attempting to take part in the world of social media?

### Racism and social media: football's response

Officials from the PFA tour the country before each season to provide advice sessions to its members. Advice on using social media is now a crucial part of these sessions. Bobby Barnes, deputy chairman of the PFA, said:

> Players need to remember when they tweet stuff it is not just going to their mates but being published for anyone to see. My advice about social media is what I would say about any form of media – don't say anything on it that you wouldn't say to someone's face if they were sitting in front of you.
>
> (Interview 2013)

In its advice the PFA reminds players that social media postings are covered by their employment contracts and that anything deemed to bring their club or the game into disrepute could lead to a ban, fine or even dismissal. While contracts allow players to respond to public or media criticism of them, this must be done in a 'responsible' manner.

Among the potential positive uses of social media by its players, the PFA cites the ability to build links and with fans, to release useful information, to boost the image of themselves and their clubs, and to promote commercial ventures. Among the potential negative outcomes are that messages may be misinterpreted or misreported, or that misjudged messages may damage a player's public image and lead to criticism. In a list of specific advice, the PFA recommends:

- Avoiding posting controversial or sensitive material.
- Avoiding comment on team or injury news.
- Avoiding criticism of others.
- Being certain of the accuracy of information.
- Being wary of posting in the heat of the moment
- Remembering that once a message is posted it is published and permanent.

(PFA 2013)

What is notably missing from the information is advice about how to handle abuse received on social media sites. In an attempt to plug this gap, the PFA have been working with the police and anti-racism campaign groups to improve the mechanisms for players to report racist abuse. Among the measures proposed are new Apps allowing players to report abuse quickly and directly to the campaign group Kick It Out, which would then take action on the player's behalf.

Simone Pound, equalities officer for the PFA, acknowledged it had more to do in this area. She said:

I think we all realise that social media poses a number of real problems. Everyone is still learning on this issue and it's a bit of a minefield. It's something that is on our radar and it's a new area. At the PFA we obviously want to protect our members. At one time some people were throwing bananas at footballers and now they're sending tweets. It's important that we address this issue.

(Interview 5 March 2013)

The FA has also made moves to try to address how footballers engage with social media. In terms of discipline, comments made on social media are charged under section E3 of the FA rules, and this has been made clear to clubs and players. The rule states:

3 (1) A Participant shall at all times act in the best interests of the game and shall not act in any manner which is improper or brings the game into disrepute or use any one, or a combination of, violent conduct, serious foul play, threatening, abusive, indecent or insulting words or behaviour.

If the comments are deemed to be racist in nature they would be additionally charged under section 3 (2), which states:

> (2) In the event of any breach of Rule E 3(1) including a reference to any one or more of a person's ethnic origin, colour, race, nationality, faith, gender, sexual orientation or disability (an 'aggravating factor'), a Regulatory Commission shall consider the imposition of an increased sanction.

If it is a player's first such offence the additional punishment is double what the sanction would have been without the aggravating factor of 'race'. For a second offence it would be treble the punishment, and for a third offence it could mean permanent suspension.

In its guidelines for players the FA makes clear that players are responsible for all postings on their social media accounts and that the rules cover re-tweets as well as original material. The FA also state that removing a post will not prevent disciplinary action from taking place if it is deemed an offence has been committed. Late in 2012, the FA also included social media in a new code of conduct applying to England international players. Among its rules, it banned the publication on Twitter or Facebook of anything which might cause embarrassment to a member of the FA, England squad or management. It also prohibited the posting of Twitter or Facebook comments on the day of a match and the day before (The Telegraph Online 17 October 2012).

Recent research shows that many football club press officers feel there is a lack of coherent and clear guidance about social media from the football authorities (Price *et al.* 2013a). There is evidence here to suggest that the PFA and FA acknowledge this and are making some attempts to improve the clarity and quality of their procedures around social media. This involves providing clearer guidelines and support on using social media, being consistent and clear about disciplinary proceedings, and providing new and more effective mechanisms for responding to abuse. Clarke Carlisle, former chairman of the PFA, acknowledges that more needs to be done:

> The level of support and advice given to footballers on these issues is growing, but as of yet it isn't comprehensive. There are guidelines issued by clubs, the union and the FA, but it can be rather ambiguous. I feel that if clubs and the FA are going to fine/punish players according to their use of social media, then the rules of use need to be stipulated in no uncertain terms. The problem with this is that it proffers questions of free speech and restrictions of it.
>
> (Interview 4 September 2013)

As hinted at by Carlisle, while the football authorities could perhaps do more on this issue, there is only so much they can do. Much responsibility in this area lies with other authorities such as the government, police, CPS and the owners of social media themselves.

## Conclusion

Football has seen some of the most high profile cases of racist abuse on social media and some of the most severe punishments dished out to offenders. The case of Liam Stacey, who was sent to prison for his comments, has provoked much public discussion about the causes of such abuse and how best to deal with it. While some argue that people should not face criminal charges for comments made on social media, no matter how offensive, others see prosecution as an important means of deterring others from similar action. Some previous research suggests legal sanctions have the potential to deter people from expressions of racism by adding to the social norms against such acts (Bodenhausen *et al.* 2009; Plant and Devine 1998). However, this is only likely to be effective if potential offenders feel there is a genuine likelihood of them being prosecuted. If people see a mountain of abuse online, but only a handful of prosecutions, it could be argued that they are less likely to feel disinhibited in their actions. As Crandall and Eshleman (2003) have identified, expressions of prejudice are more likely in situations where accountability is not thought to exist.

On the evidence of the cases discussed above, there are a variety of factors at work here. It is too simplistic to say that social media can provide anonymity and therefore makes some people more likely to be racist. In a number of the discussed cases, offenders made no attempt to hide their identities. They may have unconsciously felt safe and 'backstage' (Feagin 2010), but made no conscious effort to cloak themselves from others.

There were broadly two types of cases. In some cases, individuals seemingly act on impulse, responding quickly to banter and online chat. In many of these cases alcohol had been consumed. Such cases display a number of factors researchers have identified as diminishing an ability to suppress racist behaviour (see Chapter 4). These include rushed responses (Bodenhausen *et al.* 2009), stress or fatigue (Crandall and Eshleman 2003) and intoxication (Steele and Southwick 1985; Steele and Josephs 1990). The second type of case involves a more calculated process of snaring and provoking a victim in front of a mass audience. Such actions seem to fit with research suggesting some expressions of prejudice are linked to a need for attention (C. Bell 1980) and desire to boost self esteem (Zarate 2009). Here we have prejudice as performance for which social media provides a potentially global audience.

As we have seen, footballers have been publishers as well of victims of such prejudice. The players in question have displayed similar traits of either impulsive, unguarded behaviour or a desire to 'play' for an audience. The quality of support and advice provided for these players has been open to question. There is evidence though that after a slow start the football authorities, supported by campaign groups such as Kick It Out, are starting to get their act together. There are now guidelines for players on how to behave on social media provided by the FA and PFA, and an App for reporting racist abuse. But the authorities themselves admit that they are learning as they go on this complex and relatively new issue. A start has been made but more needs to be done. Only some of this can be done by football itself and the sport, along with others, is looking to the wider society to help it tackle these problems.

# 6   Cricket, racism and social media

## Introduction

> Horrible how many pakis are at the cricket everyone of them from here aswell should blow them all up
>
> You know there's something wrong with our country when there's more Indians at the cricket than English
>
> Can all then Indians fuck off back to India now? Instead of sponging of this country then not supporting it! #Wankers
>
> All these Indians celebrating about winning I bet most of them live in this country #fuckoff
>
> Now you Indians can fuck off back to where you came from
>
> Oh fuck off cunts, look at all the Indians in the crowed! Don't celebrate in our county, fuck off back to your shit hole
>
> Fuck off you English/Indians! Want to be Indian, go back to India!)

These tweets, posted in the space of a few hours on the evening of India's victory over England in the final of the Champions Trophy one-day international tournament at Edgbaston, Birmingham in June 2013, are evidence that cricket-related social media can be a powerful vehicle for post-colonial tensions, cultural stereotyping and basic racism specifically born as much of the game's uniquely imperialist past as its relatively egalitarian yet complex present. This chapter will seek to analyse how the discourse of issues of 'race' and national identity is evolving – or, arguably, degenerating – within the contemporary relationship between cricket and Twitter, citing specific examples of racially, culturally and symbolically antagonistic tweets, and setting them alongside previous benchmarks of 'racism' within, and as measured by, the traditional cricket media.


## Boof! Aussies going the whole Hogg

When Gemmell (2007: 1) cited 'the link to the Commonwealth' as the reason why 'cricketing discourse will always be held in the shadow of race', he may not have imagined that a platform as immediate, seemingly universal and largely uncensored as Twitter would so soon offer free rein to those arguing at the very extremes of that debate.

That one such extreme voice, the former Australian Test cricketer Rodney Hogg, was widely heard the morning after that Champions Trophy final is instructive in itself. The reason why the mainstream cricket media publicised his opinion – it was on the appointment of Darren Lehmann as Australia's new national coach – no less so. Also of relevance here is that Hogg's immediate and animated backing for Lehmann, nicknamed 'Boof', ahead of Australia's Ashes Test series against England was delivered on Twitter. 'Panic stations within English team. Boof's success and knowledge in UK makes Aussies a greater prospect'.

Hogg had been more forthright still in January 2012, when he tweeted: 'Just put out my aussie flag for Australia Day but I wasn't sure if it would offend Muslims … So I wrote "Allah is a shit" on it to make sure'. Yes, Hogg apologised, but in a manner – tweeting 'Bad attempted Australian humour, sorry if I offended you' – familiar to those who have long argued Australian culture remains mired in something similar to 1950s Britain's 'monolithic' mindset in matters of race, as perceived by W. James (1993: 240), in which all immigrants, no matter their point of origin, were regarded simply as black. As Farquharson and Marjoribanks (2006) observed, it follows that the common Australian regard for cricketers of black and Asian origin is that of an 'undifferentiated racial group', and informed by 'a larger historical discourse of white colonialism and supremacy'.

In that context, it is grimly appropriate that Hogg, a 'brilliant student of cricket' according to an editorial in the Australian *Daily Telegraph* on Lehmann's appointment, should speak up on behalf of a player who was the first cricketer suspended by the International Cricket Council for racist abuse, having called Sri Lankan opponents 'black cunts' during a one-day international in 2003. Yet the Australian media's general embrace of Lehmann's appointment a decade later was arguably more indicative still of the nation's anachronistic attitude to 'race' and national identity.

For within those paradigms, Hogg and Lehmann fit the 'bloke' profile of the white Australian male which Australia itself not reluctantly presents to the world, within which the brand of 'humour' alluded to by Hogg is enshrined. Elder (2008: 34) identified that the type of claim made by Walsh (1985) that 'the ultimate accolade in Australia is to be a "good bloke"' remains an accurate measure of white Australian national identity, within which humour helps to drive what the author Malcolm Knox (2003) described as the 'unwitting racism' which proves Australia is still not yet at a 'stage of cultural maturity where we even know what racism is'.

A decade on, with Jason Gillespie remaining the only player of Aboriginal origin to represent Australia in Test cricket, Lehmann's appointment as Australian coach endorsed by the Melbourne *Herald Sun* because 'he smokes and loves a beer. He chats. He's accessible. He speaks a language cricketers understand' (Hayes 2013), and Hogg's opinions still regarded as authoritative, does that 'good bloke' have any reason to grow up?

However, that umbilical link between 'humour' and racism may at least partly explain the relative lack of overt racism in evidence in Australian sport and, specifically, among Australian sports fans using social media. For example, the emergence of Usman Khawaja (who, it should be noted, flourished under Lehmann's coaching of the Queensland state team) as Australia's first Muslim Test cricketer in 2011 met with a largely temperate response, as did news of the attempt to fast-track the citizenship application of another Pakistan-born player, Fawad Ahmed, ahead of the 2013 Ashes series. However, a few days ahead of the Ahmed debate, the potential of 'unwitting racism' to inflame social media discourse had become evident in the antagonistic aftermath of Australian Football League club Collingwood president Eddie McGuire's suggestion that Sydney Swans player Adam Goodes, an indigenous Australian, should promote a new theatre musical production of King Kong.

One of McGuire's own players, Harry O'Brien – born in Rio de Janeiro to a Brazilian mother and a Congolese father – tweeted: 'To me Australia is very casual with racism, I would argue that many people in this country would not think what Eddie ... said last Friday is "bad"'. Tweeted responses to O'Brien ranged from 'get off your high horse ... Eddie was just using topical comedy, not being racist' to 'oi Harry ya fucken dog. Your a cunt. Dead set a big black cunt. Pull ya head in Eddie was havin fun'.

The following day, O'Brien told the *Herald Sun* newspaper: 'Every day I will experience a form of racial discrimination, whether it is through social media or walking on the street' (Smart 2013).

It was not until several months later that Fawad Ahmed could claim empathy with O'Brien and other non-white victims of Australian 'good bloke' humour. Having received Australian citizenship and made his Australia debut in a one-day international against England in August 2013, Ahmed's request to be excused from wearing a brewing company's logo on his Australia shirt prompted the following tweet from @RichieBenaud (a parody account with no link to the world-famous TV commentator of the same name): 'Fawad Ahmed rejects the VB logo on his shirt on religious grounds. @profdeano reporting he has replaced it with a major brand of explosives'.

While that specific claim against @profdeano – former Australia player Dean Jones – was untrue, it was an allusion to Jones' sacking by Indian-based TV channel Ten Sports in 2006 after he was heard on microphone saying 'The terrorist has got another wicket!' in reference to bearded Muslim South African player Hamish Amla.

Cricket Australia, the sport's national governing body, immediately condemned the @RichieBenaud tweet, a response with an enduring resonance, given that Cricket Australia itself would tweet – and hurriedly delete – a picture of four Sikh men wearing Teletubbies costumes along with the question 'Will the real Monty Panesar please stand up?! #Ashes' during the Ashes series in Australia in December 2013. A week before that tweet, Cricket Australia sacked a public address announcer for allegedly using an Indian accent when introducing Panesar, a Sikh, during one of England's Test warm-up matches less than a week before.

## England, 'our' England?

Yet, of course, all such discourse in Australia is informed by a past built on subjugation – cultural and legislative – of its indigenous population atop a platform laid by Britain's empire-builders, who 'brandished bat and ball as cultural tools with which (as they saw it) to civilize their new subjects' (Farrington *et al.* 2012: 85) throughout the colonies, driven by the 'paternalistic racism with which Britain uniformly imposed her socio-cultural mores on indigenous peoples she saw as requiring rescue from themselves' (ibid.). In cricketing terms, those mores translate to the anachronistic but enduring concept of English 'fair play'.

Today, issues such as Islamophobia, cultural stereotyping and shifting national identities clearly instruct post-colonial cricketing narrative worldwide, on social media and elsewhere. This was witnessed in the Twitter storm over the sight of British Asian fans celebrating an Indian win – in the aforementioned Champions Trophy final – over England on English soil, a contemporary antagonism partly rooted in a specific debate begun by British Conservative MP Norman Tebbit in 1990, in which he promoted the idea of a 'cricket test' as a measure of a 'large proportion' of British Asians' commitment to an itself notional British way of life. 'Are you still harking back to where you came from or where you are?' asked Tebbit in an article in the *Los Angeles Times* (Fisher 1990), in response to passionate shows of support for Pakistan and Sri Lanka – as well as Indian – touring teams.

However, given that cricket as a tool of empire has ultimately brought empowerment and a heightened or even new sense of national identity, as discussed by James (1963), Barnes (1990), Holden (2008) and Vyas (2008), to the colonies through success on the field, is the England supporters' social media spite towards India fans also informed – if only sub-consciously – by a sense of 'fair play', or more specifically the traditional colonial order of things, being usurped?

That particular sub-text would extend a pattern evident for several decades, from when the mediated UK representation of West Indies cricket fans quickly evolved – or regressed – from the relaxed but itself patronisingly stereotypical 'calypso' image to that of a menacing mob – age-old 'polar stereotypical images of black men as aggressive, yet lazy' (Marchioro 2001) – during their national team's unprecedented and unforgiving humiliation of England on English soil in the Test series of 1976. It can also be read into the provocative reporting of the increasing enmity between the England and Pakistan teams of the late 1980s and early 1990s (when the word 'Paki' appeared on back page headlines in the *Daily Mirror*), and a concurrent debate regarding national identity rooted in England's then-emerging reliance on overseas-born players. The common thread behind that media coverage, other than racial and cultural stereotyping, was England's declining performances.

The contemporary era may have seen England – ironically, with strong contributions from foreign-born players – regain significant standing in the world game. But the abuse aimed via social media at British Asian fans celebrating an Indian win over England on English soil in 2013 carried strong echoes of that former media narrative, as well as Tebbit's Enoch Powell-esque polemicising.

That it either did not occur to those who tweeted abuse that the vast majority of those backing India at Edgbaston in 2013 will have been born in Britain, or simply cut no ice with them, was not the only more contemporary sustenance for Tebbit's divisive talk of a dangerously divided Britain. He himself claimed that the implementation of a 'cricket test' might have prevented the 7/7 terrorist bombings in London in July 2005, themselves a reminder of the wider post-9/11 western angst in which cricket, as a potential platform for Islamophobia, sits.

That potential, as highlighted by Burdsey (2010) and Farrington *et al.* (2012), has been realised in recent stereotypical western media discourse on subjects such as the case of three Pakistan cricketers found guilty of 'spot-fixing' in Test matches against England in 2010, the attack on the Sri Lanka team bus – which killed seven people – in the Pakistan city of Lahore in 2009 and the sudden death of then-Pakistan coach Bob Woolmer in 2007. Some UK press coverage of the spot-fixing case harked back to those days in the early 1990s when the aforementioned *Mirror* headline dismissed fast bowlers Wasim Akram and Waqar Younis as 'Paki cheats', suggesting cheating was somehow embedded within the national psyche of Pakistan rather than a cricket-wide problem (English county player Mervyn Westfield was the first cricketer to face criminal spot-fixing charges and the game's richest event, the Indian Premier League, has seen six Indian players arrested amid similar accusations in 2013). More specifically, the British press identified Islam itself as a threat to cricket, lending credibility to rumours in the *Daily Star* and elsewhere that Woolmer had been murdered by 'Islamic fanatics' (he was later found to have suffered a heart attack), pondering whether the Muslim mindset was incompatible with the mentality required of a successful international cricketer (Slot 2007), and even suggesting a link between Pakistan cricket, match-fixing and terrorism in the case of the Sri Lankan team attack.

Despite such provocative invective, and the high-profile abuse of footballers on the same platform, there is little sign of a purely cricket-centric Islamophobic narrative on Twitter. Cricket discussion forums, particularly those based in India – where the term 'Paki' (despite its wide use in Britain as a derogatorily homogenous description for South Asians per se) has some measure of social acceptance, and socio-cultural, religious and territorial tensions have fermented throughout the 66 years following partition – have seen a spike in abusive 'Paki...' references since the spot-fixing case of 2010, while YouTube videos featuring the players involved routinely attract racist audience responses. Yet those are largely anonymous environments that could be interpreted as evidence of a growing awareness among social media users of the relative risks, as illustrated by the now numerous criminal prosecutions brought in the UK against authors of racist tweets aimed at footballers, of posting such abuse on Twitter's 'open ground'. But the frenzied and racially imbued Twitter response to the murder of soldier Lee Rigby in Woolwich in May 2013 suggests otherwise. While the rise to prominence of British Asian – and particularly of British Asian Muslim – cricketers in the English game in the new Millennium has provided 'a counterpoint ... to the climate, whether within certain newspapers or society at large, of paranoia and prejudice' (Farrington *et al.* 2012: 108), it is a 'happy but partly paradoxical situation' (ibid.) unlikely to alter what Williams (2000) discovered to be a polarisation of cricket at English local league level in which British Asian players – either 'to emphasise their traditional loyalties and identities' (Williams 2000: 52) or because they felt excluded from 'white' clubs – gravitated to Asian-only teams. Further to that latter scenario, McDonald and Ugra (1998) discovered a reluctance among many white English clubs to play even friendly (i.e. non-competitive) matches against British Asian sides because they assume their players will not drink alcohol after the game

– itself further proof of the white tendency (as witnessed in the 'Paki' tweets directed at those supporting India at Edgbaston) to falsely homogenise British Asians and perpetuate a perception of Muslim 'inferiority, negativity and threat' (Richardson 2004).

More recently, however, and in what could be regarded as an inversion of the traditional post-imperial dynamic and/or further evidence of the emancipatory potential of cricket in the former colonies, Twitter has provided a platform for Indian supporters – including British Asian fans of India – to bait the former mother country in racially loaded terms.

While, as we have discussed, the white Anglo-Saxon response on social media to the sight of British Asians celebrating beating England was largely rooted in rank bigotry, a significant proportion of Indian supporters, both on Twitter and at the game itself, resorted to a form of discourse which can attract the accusation of 'reverse racism', but must be regarded against the specific backdrop of an issue such as the Tebbit test and in the incalculably wider context of India's 89 years of yoke under the Raj and centuries more in economic subservience to the British East India Company. In other words, against the living definition of the narrative of racism as argued by Cazenave and Maddern (1999), Wellman (1977) and others as a manifestation of prejudice and systemic, societal white privilege, which itself finds a mirror in socio-cultural tensions in contemporary Britain.

When Ravi Bopara took to the field for England at Edgbaston, and more so when he began to bowl, a noisy minority of Indian fans present assailed him with chants of 'traitor' which were echoed by numerous others on Twitter. Meanwhile, both Bopara (on Twitter) and a Sikh man vocal in his backing of England (in the crowd) were branded 'coconut' – an epithet meaning brown on the outside but white on the inside – by India supporters. Bopara was born and brought up in East London and has been involved with England teams at all age group levels since his mid-teens. Ironically, although anything but unreasonable, his boyhood idol was India's Sachin Tendulkar. It would be reassuring but too convenient to rationalise the abuse Bopara received as being a straightforward measure of India supporters' passion for a game which predominates India's sporting heritage. For added to the imperialist, post-colonial and therefore emotive history of that game in India itself is a burning sense of alienation and disenfranchisement among some British Asians which has evolved extensively even since Tebbit's incendiary invective. While the 9/11 and 7/7 bombings and their socio-cultural consequences in the UK are a ubiquitous but all too obviously relevant discourse here, racial violence had already erupted in North West England in the summer of 2001, on the same weekend that former England captain Nasser Hussain – a Muslim born in Madras – had echoed Tebbit in criticising British Asians who supported India, Pakistan or Sri Lanka against

England, seemingly blind to Williams' (2000) definitive perception of British Asian-only cricket clubs as an indication of how 'Asians are in many ways outside the mainstream of popular culture in England' (ibid.). A significant difference now is that those people possess, through social media, a means of making their voices audible to the mainstream, and aimed at targets other than Bopara.

## Aggro for Aggers

Former England opening bowler Jonathan Agnew is the BBC's premier cricket commentator. Anchoring the iconic Test Match Special (TMS) programme and blogging on the BBC Sport website, Agnew is arguably the most authoritative – and certainly the most widely heard (TMS, in the digital age, has a global platform) – voice in English cricket. Beyond the airwaves, he also maintains an active presence on Twitter.

TMS has run since 1957, a longevity which 'tells of the BBC's understanding of its own power to speak of, and for – rather than visually show – England and Englishness through cricketing commentary (about players, places, cream cakes and crowd action/in-action), and a set of familiar voices' (Westall 2012). That the voices of Agnew and previous lead commentators were polished at English public schools probably also reinforces the narrative that cricket 'represents England's idealised image of itself' (ibid.). Moreover, as Agnew himself can testify, it renders them and TMS in general, vulnerable to accusations of post-colonial, pro-England bias, despite the permanent presence of a range of overseas former players in the TMS commentary box.

In August 2011, as England looked to close out a comprehensive 4–0 home Test series win over India in the final match at The Oval, an incident involving the tourists' veteran batsman Rahul Dravid sparked a controversy which resulted in Agnew being targeted on Twitter.

Dravid was given out caught, although TV replays suggested that his bat had not made contact with the ball. The player himself admitted afterwards that he thought he had hit the ball, prompting Agnew to publicly support the decision. That in turn led to Agnew becoming the subject of a stream of tweets from Indian fans on Twitter which were 'abusive, but also racist in tone. Racist, in a way that if I said that to an Indian, I would quite rightly be condemned' (Interview 25 June 2013). Agnew was perturbed enough by the experience to go public about it.

Agnew (Interview 25 June 2013) adds:

> To suggest that I am what I am because I'm white, or that I'm making the statements I'm making because I'm white or because I'm English or

because I'm biased … that's totally out of order. The problem with India – and this was the issue in that year – is there's a bit of a language issue that perhaps meant people tweeting abuse weren't aware of quite how offensive they were being. I think, as well, a lot of people were new to it themselves, and so I don't think they knew the boundaries, perhaps. They've suddenly got access to people, and this very ignorant minority thought: 'Here we go, here's the chance to slag a few well known people off. This is good sport'.

There is an argument that Agnew may be – in cricketing parlance – on a sticky wicket in his critique of social media methodology, if not penetration, in India. More than a year before he was targeted over the Dravid affair, India could claim 8.2 per cent of Twitter's worldwide user base – a figure second only to the United States. By July 2013, India had almost 20 million Twitter users. Conversely, though, that 20 million represents less than 2 per cent of the nation's population, an estimated 88 per cent of whom have no internet access.

Agnew does not offer up examples of the 'racist' tweets he received in 2011, and hesitates to apportion their content to post-colonial resentments, saying: 'I don't know. I'd prefer to think that that sort of criticism is born of frustration at that person's team not playing well' (Interview 25 June 2013). However, that theory is challenged not only by popular critical discourse regarding 'reverse racism', but by a tweet – since deleted – replying to a post by the popular Twitter account @AltCricket in November 2012, during England's winter tour of India, which read: 'Agnew is racist scum – should go back to Britain and join rest of scum in national front – no manners get out of india'.

Interestingly, and ironically, the tweet by @AltCricket which prompted that response was a criticism of the mechanism of dealing with abusive tweets which Agnew (Interview 25 June 2013) adopted as a consequence of his experience with India supporters:

My rule with Twitter is that you wouldn't say anything on Twitter – or anywhere else – that you wouldn't say to somebody's face. I've become a much more virulent blocker of people now than I was then [in August 2011] … now I just don't give people a second chance. If someone sends me a message that I consider to be rude, offensive and disrespectful, and that they wouldn't say to my face, they'll get no reply. I think it's wrong to retweet [abuse], so I try not to do that, although it's tempting sometimes. I try not to do that because then 'they' sort of win, so I just block it quietly and move on. That's my rule, that's the way – and why – I do it, and I tend not to let people back again.

@AltCricket argued Agnew's method 'defeats the object of Twitter. If you didn't want spaghetti then why'd you come to Italy?'

Setting aside the white privilege issue and the consequent theory, as put forward by Anderson (2010), Fish (1993), Wise (2002) and others, that 'reverse racism' cannot exist, Agnew's affront at the abuse he received is genuine, and the relationship he has since enjoyed with the very large majority of Indian cricket supporters he interacts with – on Twitter and elsewhere – is cordial enough to both lend the lie to accusations of bias and support his belief in a positive evolution of behaviour on social media. 'I think every month on Twitter is like a new experience, and that was two years ago, so I think everybody has moved on a lot since then.'

## Bumble's fumbles

However, the example of another cricket broadcaster, David Lloyd, suggests Jonathan Agnew's improved social media experience is down to his management of the medium rather than any sudden settling of post-colonial scores.

Lloyd is a commentator on Sky Sports TV and a former England Test player. His Lancastrian brogue, lugubrious to some watchers of English cricket but mellifluous to many others who view him as an amiable anachronism, 'in which vowels are rolled around the mouth like a vintage claret' (White 2013), and his stock of catchphrases are a distraction from the distinctly politically incorrect nature of some of his broadcast output since he swapped coaching – he took charge of the England team between 1996 and 1999 – for the commentary box. Yet it is on Twitter – 'it's an illness – I'm addicted ... But I love it for the wind-up' (ibid.) – where he has caused particular friction.

For it is South Asian cricket fans who have been most irked by Lloyd – popularly known as Bumble (after an old children's TV show, rather than any cricketing or commentating faux pas) – on Twitter. That avuncular-sounding nickname seems appropriate for much of his social media output, which could be described as gentle ribbing – self-deprecation included – rather than provocative invective. ' "It's not malice. It's mischief, double entendre. That's what I am: mischievous". As anyone who follows him on Twitter ... endlessly provoking Indian cricket fans, will testify' (ibid.). However, during the summer of 2013, Lloyd's discourse – with India fans and others he *assumed* to be India fans – become increasingly antagonistic and, at times, evoked a sub-text redolent of both the 'Tebbit test' of old and contemporary socio-cultural tensions.

In that summer's opening Test match between England and Australia at Trent Bridge, England's Stuart Broad was widely criticised for refusing to 'walk' – i.e. end his innings voluntarily – when the umpires mistakenly gave him not out despite him clearly having edged a ball which was caught at slip. Amid the subsequent debate, Lloyd supported Broad on the basis that very few modern professional cricketers 'walk' in such a situation, prompting this tweet: '@Adeelk007 @BumbleCricket Shut up bumble, I can't believe sky sports recruit such bias commentators! The lot of u alone overhype every English player'.

Lloyd tweeted back: '@Adeelk007 terrific game … thanks for your interest and comments … how is Err … London tonight? #chiponbothshoulders'.

In response, @Adeelk007 pointed out: 'yes I'm a Londoner, and I support England…'

The original tweet by @Adeelk007 was perhaps also informed by Lloyd's equally marked lack of support for a batsman who refused to 'walk' during a match between India and Pakistan during the Champions Trophy tournament, played in England in June 2013, when he tweeted a plea for more 'honesty' from players.

However, there was seemingly less ambiguity about Lloyd's part in a Twitter exchange with @aqib96 (later @aqib96pd), apparently a Pakistan supporter, in February 2012 during England's Test, one-day international and Twenty20 series against Pakistan in Dubai and Abu Dhabi. While the context of the interaction appears to be Lloyd responding to sustained abuse (@aqib96's tweets during that period are unrecorded), the tenor of his replies – to someone he discovers during their 'conversation' is a British Pakistani teenager living in Walsall, England – is instructive.

> BumbleCricket: @Aqib96
> hi Aqib wouldn't come to Eng til it warms up You will need a Visa being Indian

> BumbleCricket: @Aqib96
> ah not racism again! Aqib You can do better than that Come to Eng Lots love it here

> BumbleCricket: @Aqib96
> A British Pakistani? So you have been to Eng? Hope you enjoyed it. Suppose you back home now in Karachi or maybe Multan

> BumbleCricket: @Aqib96
> Ah just seen you in Walsall Are you on holiday before going back to Pakistan … nice Walsall
> @aqib96 multi national country. You should come over Lots do Seem to love it for some reason

BumbleCricket: @Aqib96 Aqib
Have you noticed I can hold a conversation without bad language? Still, don't suppose you been here long

BumbleCricket: @Aqib96 just helping you out It's called English ... seeing you not been here long, justing helping

BumbleCricket: @aqib96 Aqib
Did mr Patel call you about the lettuce? How is Jennifer?

Seemingly blunt social typecasting (is Lloyd referring to the clichéd UK 'corner shop' in his final tweet?), the monolithically British depiction of South Asians as a homogenous 'Other', and the consequent, underlying but equally familiar and crude 'go back home' message – such a narrative, delivered in whatever context, covers almost the gamut of racial and cultural stereotyping and more than nods to the 'pervasive image of Otherness' (Burdsey 2010: 316) as most notably discussed by Said (1985).

Indeed, 15 months later, Lloyd offered a sense of his wider perspective on 'Otherness', when responding on Twitter to the murder of British soldier Lee Rigby in Woolwich, London.

In the hours following the killing, Lloyd tweeted: 'London mayor says, "far too early to draw conclusions" re Woolwich ... Idiot'.

Urged by a Twitter user to then 'wait for facts before the blame game starts', Lloyd responded: 'FACTS!!!! Staring you in the face!!'

He then tweeted: 'Woolwich ... Perpetrators ... Name names ... And where are they from?'

Amid a febrile atmosphere, Lloyd's words found favour with the British far right, with some of his most strident support on Twitter voiced by users posting under pseudonyms such as 'NO SURRENDER!' and consisting of responses such as 'bumble fck these half breeds off, how the fck can talk shit like this #wankers'. When challenged to defend his intimation ('Woolwich ... Treatment for attackers ... ???') that fusilier Rigby's suspected killers should have been left to die in the street after being shot and wounded by police, Lloyd replied sardonically: 'you prob right ... Long drawn out court case ... Appeals ... etc etc etc etc'.

Taken in isolation, given the spike in community tensions and raw anger across Britain immediately after the Woolwich incident, Lloyd's tweets might be measured against their context. Similarly, his regular Twitter jousts with India fans can, in themselves, be passed off as banter. Set alongside his 'mr Patel', 'back home now in Karachi' and 'justing helping' barbs, however, and they constitute a consistency of narrative which might be much less easily excused. Not that Sky TV, for whom Lloyd continues to work, appear to have asked him for excuses. It should also be noted that both Lee Rigby's murderers were born in London. Come July 2013, another Twitter user, @VijaysinghDeol cast his verdict on Lloyd: 'Hey POMmy.Shut the fuck uppp Bitch.... You colonial racist ... Fuck ur ancestors'. Lloyd's response? 'Check this warrior'.

Although Agnew's approach to Twitter has always been infinitely more circumspect, the not dissimilar abuse he has received from supporters of Asian sides has sharpened his reflexive cognition – and apprehension – of the incendiary potential of the type of interaction beloved of Lloyd, not least when it relates to Pakistan and its cricket team, whose treatment during the last two decades by the UK press has been imbued with 'age-old stereotypes within what was formerly known as the "East" is a sociological and cultural opposite – and poor relation – of the West' (Farrington *et al.* 2012: 103) since long before the socio-cultural tensions stirred up by 9/11 and 7/7, let alone the spot-fixing scandal of 2011 which saw three Pakistan players and a player's agent jailed. Agnew says:

> I think there'll always be the opportunity for certain people to do certain things [on Twitter]. I mean passions often run high. If you look at something like the situation with the Pakistan team in 2006 [playing against England] at The Oval, when the questions were being asked 'were they ball tampering, were they not ball-tampering?' and they didn't come out to play after tea. If that had been in 'Twitterland' in the Twitter era, I suspect that would have incited quite a lot. So you just hope that people will take a deep breath, and of course you mustn't say anything inflammatory yourself; and hopefully I don't because what annoys me more than anything is this accusation of bias. That really annoys me. I am not biased. I am as likely to criticise an English cricketer as I am a Pakistani cricketer. So that always gets me. Is there a post-colonial element to it? I don't know. I'd prefer to think that that sort of criticism is born of frustration at that person's team not playing well.

## Against Islam, not individuals?

Whatever engenders resentment in South Asia towards the England cricket team and its media, cricket's appropriation as a platform for Islamophobia – by sections of the 'white' media and through 'white' social discourse – has been well documented by Williams, Farrington *et al.*, Searle and others. Despite this – and, indeed, the harsh experience and treatment of the likes of British boxer Amir Khan on Twitter (see Chapter 7) – social media has not yet been widely used to target Muslim cricketers as individuals.

Such was Usman Khawaja's poor form against England in the summer of 2013, such is Australia's history of racist discourse and such is the kneejerk immediacy of Twitter, it might be assumed that the lineage and faith of a Muslim player born in Pakistan would be implicated by some in his sub-standard performances. However, Australian Twitter users did not make that link. Instead, it was an English cricket journalist, the *Sunday Telegraph*'s Scyld Berry, who suggested that Khawaja had been selected on anything but merit. In predicting, after the fourth Ashes Test of the summer of 2013, that Khawaja would be dropped, Berry wrote: 'Australia's experiment with their Asian immigrant population will be shelved'.

In any case, cricket-related antagonism towards Muslims on social media is not a 'white' preserve. Many derogative 'Paki'-tagged tweets, while clearly not alluding to a homogenous South Asian 'Other', are posted by Indian supporters; in whose narrative post-partition prejudices – religious (Hindu and/or Sikh versus Muslim), socio-cultural (courtesy of the British Raj-endorsed caste system and the modern shadow of terrorism) and sport-ing (Pakistan's cricket team has faced sanctions and restrictions when playing in India in recent years) – are writ large.

On the day of India's Champions Trophy final against England, ten tour-ists were shot dead at the base camp of the Nanga Parbat mountain in North West Pakistan in an attack for which the Pakistani Taliban admitted respons-ibility, prompting tweets such as this: 'Dif B/W India and Pakistan … India is playing the final of #CR2013 New Super Power of Cricket. Pakis Killing Tourists to save Islam'. Another Indian fan, upon seeing Pakistan supporters talking down India's victory prospects when interviewed for TV on the day of the game, tweeted: 'These pakis on sky sports news would be supporting England at the cricket, cuz their own team is full of cheaters #teamindia'.

In that final respect, the depiction of corruption in cricket and Islamist fundamentalism as somehow 'shared cultural signifiers' (Farrington *et al.* 2012) in Pakistan is as common in India as it is in the right-leaning UK press, which has long insinuated – or imagined – a link between fatwas and match-fixing, and even suggested that Pakistani cricket has been complicit in terrorism (in the case of the attack on the Sri Lanka team bus in Lahore in 2007). At which point, it is necessary to consider India's own litany of crick-eting corruption, founded on an established network of corrupt Indian book-makers implicated in betting scams worldwide, along with the fact that the first cricketer charged in a criminal court for 'spot-fixing' (he admitted to deliberately conceding runs) was an Englishman, Mervyn Westfield.

However, as elsewhere, the dynamic of cricket-centric Indian prejudices – most often, Islamophobia – on Twitter leans towards abuse not of individuals but of collectives; and while such abuse is informed by the historical and contemporary issues mentioned above, India's increasing cricketing hege-mony, not merely in South Asia, but – in financial terms at least – world-wide, is arguably a concomitant factor, with the Indian Premier League well established as the game's most lucrative competition and its highest governing body, the International Cricket Council, consequently dominated by Indian administrators.

Within that context, and given his belief that India is 'a tribal society ... that cannot examine individuals without the prejudice of a collective label', the Indian journalist Aakar Patel argues:

> The other thing to observe is that we find nothing wrong in behaving like schoolyard bullies, and at the same time, spout clichés about cricket being a gentleman's game. It's nothing of the sort in India. It's like a circus in Rome: vicious and nationalistic. Why are we so petty and mean? The answer is because we can be. We kick around smaller nations that are our neighbours because we can...

For India 2013, read Britain's empire builders of the nineteenth century? If India is now playing the role of the colonial bully, that cricket – an imperial tool of subjugation which became 'a byword for the fight for emancipation from the Mother Country' (Farrington *et al.* 2012: 86) – should offer its stage and script is grimly ironic. Still more so, notwithstanding Aakar Patel's contemporary assessment, because cricket itself – as 'the new cultural institution by which England sought to socialize the populations and reinforce hierarchies in its colonies' (McClendon 1998) – helped to create the caste hegemony of Hindus over Muslims during the British Raj which would shape the cultural landscapes, and entrench the mutual enmities, of post-partition India and Pakistan.

And yet, and yet...

In July 2013, the selection of Parvez Rasool for the India cricket squad – the first ever call-up of a Kashmiri Muslim player – produced a telling social media measure of India's conflicting treatment of collective and individual 'Others'. Against the backdrop of a bitter and often bloody territorial dispute between India and Pakistan, whose thwarted claim to governance of almost all of Kashmir (Pakistan holds around one-third of the region) has become a cause celebre for Muslims worldwide, Rasool – who hails from Jammu, an area particularly synonymous with the Kashmiri conflict and a frequent target for insurgent attacks against the Indian administration – was picked in the squad for India's one-day international series against Zimbabwe. Already infused by Kashmir's turbulent modern history, Rasool's selection was also loaded with personal, socio-cultural and religious symbolism, not least because of his detainment by police in a hotel in the Indian city of Bangalore in 2009 on suspicion of being a terrorist, after he objected on religious grounds to sniffer dogs checking his cricket bag (which contained a copy of the Koran and a Muslim prayer mat).

Yet, overwhelmingly, the Indian response on Twitter to his selection was one of warm welcome rather than stereotyped suspicion or abuse, with isolated suggestions that the decision was a symbolic, politically informed sop to Kashmiri Muslims more than tempered by tweets hailing his inclusion as proof of the India team becoming a genuine meritocracy. Only within Kashmir itself, and even then only by a dissenting handful, was Rasool's promotion to the international stage given a negative spin, in tweets such as 'Everyone is discussing Parvez Rasool But For Me He Is Nothing But A Traitor May Allah Show Him'.

That said, the overarching issue of Kashmiri governance did infect Rasool-related Twitter discourse when he was then left out of the actual India team for all five matches against Zimbabwe – a decision which Kashmiri Muslim politician Omar Abdullah depicted as a calculated slap-down by tweeting 'Did you really have to take him all the way to Zimbabwe to demoralise him?? Wouldn't it have been cheaper to just do it at home???' to an angry response in India, irritating religious and socio-cultural wounds to which Rasool's original selection had applied salve.

Generally speaking, however, the treatment on Twitter of Rasool himself is suggestive again of a situation wherein the platform can be a vehicle for cricket-related prejudice, but is rarely driven at individual targets. Will that change? The question is perhaps most pertinently asked in Britain, where the public is assailed by mainstream media coverage which promotes 'white' cultural hegemony and has already drawn tenuous but highly antagonistic links between Pakistan cricketing corruption and terrorism; coverage which Lord Herman Ouseley, former chairman of the Commission for Racial Equality, believes is 'a wider reflection of the way people see Islam/Muslims in a British context' and 'used to reinforce so many other things' (Ouseley in Farrington *et al.* 2012: 108).

Academic and cricket journalist Rob Steen (also in Farrington *et al.* 2012: 109) pondered mainstream media's treatment of a player such as Moeen Ali – if, given his status as one of English county cricket's leading run scorers and premier all-round players, he was to be called up by England – and his resulting treatment by the English public.

> He's obviously a little bit more religious than most Muslim players. He's got the 'beard' and he could and should be a contender for the England one-day side at the very least over the next couple of years. I think that will be an interesting little development in terms of the way he is presented.

The prescience of those words would be proved in February 2014, when Moeen was called up to the England one-day international squad and was

dubbed 'Osama bin laden', 'Borat' and another of the England team's perceived 'foreigners' … by users on as mainstream a social media medium as
BBC Sport's Facebook page (Hodgson 2014). Yes, the first decade of this
century proved 'a watershed for British Asian players' (Farrington *et al.*
2012: 100), with numerous of them representing England in both Test and
limited-overs cricket. However, unlike Moeen, none of them were particularly, openly devout Muslims. None of them, unlike Moeen, sported a
fulsome beard. None of them, again unlike Moeen, have punctuated discussions of their career and prospects with phrases such as 'Insha'Allah' (Allah
willing) and 'Alhamdulillah' (Praise to God). Instead, the most celebrated
British Asian England players were Nasser Hussain, a Muslim who was
captain of England when he echoed Norman Tebbit in asking in 2001 why
British Asians born or brought up in the UK 'cannot support England' (cited
in Syal 2001), and Monty Panesar, a Sikh who was 'embraced by the public
… as much because of his weaknesses as his strengths' (Steen, in Farrington
*et al.* 2012: 95), and therefore whose potentially threatening 'Otherness has
been "sanitised"'' (Fletcher 2011).

When posed the litmus test of Moeen's promotion to the England side,
what price certain cricket commentators, let alone rank and file Twitter users,
falling foul of crude stereotyping or crass, 'race'-informed 'humour' in the
manner of Rodney Hogg, his former Australia team-mate Dean Jones or,
indeed, Cricket Australia?

That potential prospect, particularly since the Crown Prosecution Service
in England effectively 'raised the bar' for criminal prosecutions of abuse –
including racist abuse – on social media (see Chapter 3), begs debate on
whether proaction on behalf of English cricket's authorities, whether through
the launch of social media-specific awareness campaigns or better promotion
on social media of existing anti-racism projects, is required to guard against
British Asian cricketers suffering individual abuse similar to that experienced by boxer Amir Khan and numerous prominent black football
personalities.

However, the England and Wales Cricket Board (ECB), the chief admin-
istrative body in English cricket, is confident that the game will avoid such
difficulties. The ECB director of marketing and communications Steve
Elworthy (Interview 26 February 2013) said:

> We have an anti-racism code and zero tolerance approach to racism
> which is communicated and displayed at all major matches on the big
> screens and prominent signage in ground during matches. This also
> applies to the use of social media and our approach to the matter. We see
> the social media space as a positive innovation and we have not experi-
> enced any significant issues with racist comments in the UK…

## Conclusion

The ECB is partly justified in its assertion that social media's relationship with cricket, specifically the English game, is hitherto not as obviously problematic as that between social media and football. Only partly so, for while overtly racist abuse of individual cricketers in England – akin to that suffered by numerous footballers – on Twitter or comparable platforms is as yet rare, we have evidence that cricket, with a colonial history whose relevance continues to evolve through the prism of race, can become a social media vehicle for racism and associated contemporary tensions of culture and national identity in Britain, more so even than in South Asia, where comparable antagonisms are arguably sharper still. Indeed, to the British observers who stand in moral judgement of the anachronistic humour and culture of machismo at the heart of Australia's monolithic societal racism and the resulting forgiveness, at best, of bigoted social media comment involving 'good blokes' such as Rodney Hogg (who, although criticised, faced no professional censure for his 'Allah is a shit' tweet), the more subtly provocative but more consistent Twitter discourse of David Lloyd – who remains one of Sky TV's premier cricket commentators – should be an equally troubling, and local, concern, linking with, if not feeding, as it does the overt racism witnessed on social media when British Asians are seen and heard to celebrate their heritage by supporting India, Pakistan and other touring teams from the sub-continent inside English grounds. What price that racism – or cultural intolerance, imbued as it is with the socio-cultural hangovers from the 9/11 and 7/7 attacks, the murder of Lee Rigby and the emergence of the anti-immigration UK Independence Party in the British political mainstream – being aimed, via Twitter, at a British Asian player whose shirt bears the three lions of England but whose beard marks him out to many among a white English audience as 'Other'? Moeen Ali is already finding out.

Though rooted in modern historical disjuncture and cultural and religious unease rather than tensions specifically of 'race', the already tangible use of social media as a platform for cricket-related Indo-Pak abuse – and its potential for crystallising collective prejudices into the abuse of individuals – is also a concern which is likely to mount as social media's South Asian footprint rapidly expands.

# 7   Boxing, racism and social media

## Introduction

Amir Khan became a public name after winning a silver medal at the 2004 Athens Olympics. Aged just 17, and Britain's sole boxing representative, Khan won much public and sporting admiration for his efforts. His identity has subsequently become an amalgamation of the contemporary, the historical, the local and the global. Inspired by the great African American Muhammad Ali, and brought up supporting Bolton Wanderers in the UK, Khan, a proud British Pakistani Muslim, has become a pinnacle definer of contemporary multicultural Britain. However, for some, no matter how hard and determined Khan is to underline his hybrid identity, the thought of one of 'them' winning for 'us' is difficult to comprehend. Increasingly Khan has had to defend his actions and point out that he is a boxer, not a social political commentator. What is also increasingly noticeable is the openly racist comments about Khan that are posted online. These expressions appear to show that, for many, Khan is, and always will be, an outsider, open to racial disparagement for his ethnicity, and Islamophobic comments due to his faith. These issues will be explored in the following chapter, which analyses racist abuse of Khan across a variety of social media. While most of the focus of this book has been on social networking sites (such as Facebook and Twitter), this chapter will also bring in material from user-generated sites (such as YouTube, forums and readers' comments).

## Amir Khan and online racism

Media representations of Amir Khan can provide a useful example of the relationships between current 'race' thinking, contemporary racism and the employment of new media to articulate these assumptions. On the one hand Khan is a proud Pakistani Muslim, yet he simultaneously defines himself as British and has even been nicknamed 'the pride of Bolton'. This conditional belonging (Saeed *et al.* 1999) by Khan has made him a role model for British Muslims, while simultaneously more acceptable to the mainstream British public (Burdsey 2007). However, Burdsey (2007: 623) does not acknowledge that the acceptance of Khan hides or even consciously conceals the increased prejudice towards British Muslims in society:

> Khan is seen as filling a role in communities that are believed to lack positive role models. This serves to further position Khan as the 'acceptable' or 'desirable' face of British Islam. This stance is perhaps best epitomised by the *Daily Mail*'s Jeff Powell who, in distinguishing Khan from the 'other' Muslims that his paper continues to admonish, suggests that 'this charming son of Islam is doing the power of good for Anglo-Asian relations'.

It has been noted how Khan has been praised by the mainstream media for speaking out against terrorist attacks in London (Kilvington *et al.* 2013). This clearly suggests that being a 'good' British Muslim involves speaking out about terrorism and fundamentalism, while silence on such issues may be seen as tacit support for such behaviour (Saeed 2003, 2004). Similarly Hylton (2009: 98) notes that Khan has been represented as the good Muslim: 'The underlying message is again that "this is what you should be like to fit in" as cultural markers of Asianess are diluted for commonly accepted signifiers of Britishness'. In many respects, this resonates with the media coverage of black athletes as either role models or bad boys (Kilvington *et al.* 2013).

Whereas African Caribbeans are popularly regarded as being physically endowed with 'natural' sporting abilities (Hoberman 1997), British Asians tend to be classified as the insufficient sporting Other, lacking the physique, skill and inclination to be successful in these disciplines (Kilvington *et al.* 2013). The embedding of these now taken for granted stereotypes can be traced back to slavery, colonialism and in the context of British Asians specifically, the creation of the Raj in India. Articulating the Orientalist discourse of 'the west and the rest' (Said 1985; Hall 1996), the British portrayed themselves as a modern, civilised and potent 'race' contrasted with an indigenous Indian population who were backward, primitive and unhealthy. Within a colonial sporting frame (Carrington 2010), Asian men were seen to be physically weak and timid (Kilvington 2012). Consider the assumption behind the so called popular pastime of the 1970s, 'paki-bashing' (Saeed 2007).

Despite the fallacy of these representations and their rebuttal by athletes like Amir Khan, historical ideological myths still underpin contemporary ways of seeing this group. Khan is now one of a handful of British Asian sports stars that challenge the notion that 'Asians can do physical sport'

(Kilvington 2012). The 2013 British Asian Sports Award (BASA) of the decade was won by Khan himself. Indeed in recent years boxing has seen a massive surge in popularity amongst British Asians.

If one were to analyse the online material describing/responding to Khan's ability, lifestyle and identity one quickly sees a discourse that is dominated around issues of 'race', ethnic and national narratives and counter narratives (Saeed 2011). These arguments have taken on a global sphere with the ease of access to social and new media. Furthermore the anonymity that new media provides gives a fascinating commentary on the language of contemporary racism.

In 2011 while en route to train for a fight, Amir Khan tweeted that

> Landed in LA safe, but the customs took the – again because I'm Muslim. Kept me in some holding room for over two hours. They were so arrogant and unprofessional. Didn't know how to talk to people. Well I'm out now and it can't get any worse.
>
> (Davies 2011)

His manager was also quoted as saying that:

> Names like Khan and Muhammad are commonly stopped. There are seven levels of security threat, with seven being the highest, and Amir has come in at the full seven. His name is Khan; he is a Muslim; between visits to the United States, he visits Pakistan; and he recently went to another Muslim country, Egypt, on holiday. All these things are taken into account by US Homeland Security.
>
> (Davies 2011)

The above quotes were reported in an online article by the *Telegraph* newspaper. Like many UK national newspapers, the *Telegraph* allows readers to make online comments. While much of this book has focused on social networking sites, user generated material is relevant under a wider definition of social media (see Chapter 2 for a full discussion of this). What followed were 45 comments that discussed this issue. One reader posted a number of comments about the story and in response to other readers. The reader's name and tone suggest that 'race baiting' and ridiculing Khan's experience was his clear intention.

### Empire_Loyalist_UFF 06/10/2011 01:39 PM
So he's been there countless times and countless times he's been stopped, yet continues to go knowing he'll be stopped … and then moans about it.

Either stay at home or abide by the rules of the guest country you're visiting, in much the same way your forefathers were meant to in Bolton.

You'd have a lot more sympathy if you could bring yourself to mention the cancer that is Muslim Terror and the shame you feel by being delayed by immigration because of the actions of a lot of the people who claim to be of the same religion as yourself.

If you don't like it, set up camp in Bognor and have your fights at Butlins.

The comment clearly echoes contemporary racist discourse. People with non-white skin in Britain have habitually been designated as outsiders (or Other), as 'ethnic minorities' whose culture is alien and incompatible with that of the host nation (Saeed 2007). Furthermore, it could be suggested that the issues of asylum seekers/refugees have been conflated with the issue of (Islamic fundamentalist) terrorism to create a new form of racism. Racism, as many authors have noted, does not remain static but evolves and adapts to circumstance and situation (Mason 2000; Solomos 2003).

Hence, in this online forum, Islam is equated with terrorism and despite being UK born and representing the UK in the Olympics – Khan is told that he is merely a 'guest' in this country. Thus regardless of Khan's previous assertions of being proud to be British, his religious identity is seen as being incompatible with being British. The current climate with the ongoing 'war on terrorism' has brought Muslim minority groups into the media spotlight and adversely affected the Muslim population in the UK. New components within racist terminology appeared, and were used in a manner that could be argued were deliberately provocative to bait and ridicule Muslims and other ethnic minorities. Many social commentators have noted that media language has been fashioned in such a way as to cause many to talk about a 'criminal culture' (Poole 2002; Saeed 1999).

The perceived support among British Muslims of bin Laden, Palestinian suicide bombers and Kashmiri separatists have been further fuelled by these recent events in the North of England. The disturbances in the North of England have in some quarters been presented as a particular problem with the Muslim community and not with the British Asian community as a whole (Saeed 2004, 2007).

Pakistani and Bangladeshi communities in particular have been represented in the media as separatist, insular and unwilling to integrate with wider society. Furthermore, the old stereotypical image of 'Asian passivity' has been replaced by a more militant aggressive identity that is meant to be further at odds with 'British secular society'. The concept of 'culture clash' has been highlighted to imply that British Muslims are at odds with mainstream society (Ansari 2003; Modood 1994, 1997).

This comment also echoes the concept of trivialisation that can help marginalise and ignore the very obvious effects of racism. As Hylton has argued:

> Trivialization and minimization emerged through semantical turns, sarcasm, and pedantic arguments as the complexities of 'race' and racial politics were simplified to render them impotent and benign.... The key distinction is that trivialization politics resist the idea that racism occurred by moving to undermine, mock, or ignore its significance or consequences.
>
> (Hylton 2005: 8)

Note the initial sentence in the comment:

> So he's been there countless times and countless times he's been stopped, yet continues to go knowing he'll be stopped ... and then moans about it.

Then this world-class boxer is told:

> If you don't like it, set up camp in Bognor and have your fights at Butlins.

It is evident that this denial of racism is expounded from a position of perceived cultural privilege where racist experiences are undermined by the 'common sense' approach that tackles political correctness. These comments are not just a product of online communities but are a product of wider society. Hampton and Wellman argue that the study of virtual communities should not be restricted to interactions that take place online, but should include observations of how online interactions fit into the entire set of social ties that make up the multiple communities in which we are all involved' (1999: 12). Thus it can be argued that online life blends in with and is influenced by offline life.

Of course it could be suggested that this poster was, in Rheingold's (2000) words, a bigot or charlatan vying for public attention. Furthermore the incident itself, involving immigration officials and US homeland security, led itself to an overtly political discussion. However even when Amir Khan is involved in the sporting arena, we can see from the following discussion that it often invokes intense political discussion around debates of 'race' and religion (Burdsey 2007). A routine search on YouTube or various online boxing forums indicates a plethora of comments that display overtly racist abuse directed to Amir Khan, his fans or his ethnic/religious background. Once again, acknowledging the possibility of comments cited to provoke reactions with the knowledge that a poster identity and physical safety is virtually assured, these postings do indicate a high degree of overt racism that makes for uncomfortable reading.

For example, on a video posted on YouTube of Khan's victory of Marco Barrera (2009), the following comments were posted by YouTube users:

**IrontoughItalian**

Europeans, South Americans, Africans they have the genes with muscles and strength. The Paki/Indian gene is very weak and there penis is very small. Its fact.

How many medals have India won at the olympics with 1 billion people and then look at China how many medals the rack up with there billion. Its the weak gene

**johnosandra (sic)**

That's one thing your right on they need to slow down their population growth, its unsustainable for earth. They all have so many kids they don't have the money to feed them and expect western countries to on board unsustainable population growth. Why did we have wars? If they halve their population they're all worth twice as much. They need more abortions and contraception widely available. Poor children growing up in disgusting conditions because of human stupidity, disgusting.

Both of these comments are noteworthy in that they echo ignorance of the developing world while simultaneously alluding to biological racism. Mills (2007) has previously defined this as a facet of the performance of 'white ignorance' where the interests of whiteness are preserved through a multifaceted assortment of strategies, one of which is the practice of ignoring major social and global issues. These posts exhibit typical elements of what some scholars define as white discourse, including denial of the benefits of white privilege – the advantages a white person receives simply by being white – and the unwillingness (conscious or unconscious) to recognise the implications of institutional and epistemic racism (McKee 2002).

In April 2013, Amir Khan beat Mexican Julio Diaz on points in what was labelled one of the most exciting fights in the UK. The fight saw Khan knocked down in the fourth round but recovering to win a unanimous decision. However what followed was a discussion by boxing fans that again alluded to physical attributes of Asians and the accompanying narratives of accusations of racism/Islamophobia.

The BBC followed up the initial story entitled, 'Amir Khan: why he just can't win over the doubters' (Dirs 2013). This article begins: 'Spend an hour on Twitter after an Amir Khan fight and you will discover why the Bolton-born boxer doesn't spend more time in his home country than he strictly needs to'. This is a reference to the social media chatter that questions Khan's boxing ability along with more intense discourse that debates nation, 'race' and religion. The author is clearly a Khan admirer and also has witnessed Khan on the receiving end of racist taunts in the UK at previous fights.

What follows though are 200 comments on the BBC webpage about this article. A simple check reveals that 12 comments mentioned Khan's colour. This clearly alludes to 'race' thinking. Indeed online posters specifically mention 'race', 26 times in the forum. Furthermore, 18 comments discuss Khan's Islamic faith as a possible reason to his unpopularity, while a number of comments posted clearly indicate that Khan is a victim of racism:

5 **Sal** Khan is abused and hated by many in the UK because he is a muslim and because he is of Pakistani origin. Like it or not, that is the simple, cold & depressing truth

8. **kol** I agree Sal. Even though many people claim not to be overtly racist there is definitely a connection between being a UK Muslim and being incredibly unpopular. Out of interest has there been an incredibly popular Muslim boxer in the UK

179. **hiren** To all giving him grief about the race card – your all going on like it doesn't happen … you just have to look at Football. Welcome to Britain He's British when he's winning (Olympics) when he loosing he's a P*** He is one of the few British muslim's who younger muslims look up to – rather that than terrorism. My previous comment awaiting moderation lets see if this gets through the checks.

While overt racist abuse is 'moderated' out of the forum BBC this is replaced with a variety of comments that suggest that Khan is playing the 'race' card:

192. **Behemoth66** I do not like Khan because he uses excuses rather admit he was fairly beaten but the main reason is team Kahn hand picks 30+ year olds when they can or people with a poor KO percentage when will he fight a decent contender? Playing the race card is a poor excuse

158. **guys** It really annoys me when people feel the need to use the race card! I'm sure there are some idiots on this thread who dont like Khan because of race/religion, however, I'm sure the majority of people on here dont like him for the same reason I dont. He has this overinflated

ego after he has never really beaten anyone good apart from Maidana. Put him infront of a decent fighter and he loses.

112. **f1fan2011** @107 Hamed is from the Yemen, not Pakistan. Nigel Benn isnt white and neither is Hamed and were and still are very popular. Anyone remember a certain Mr Bruno? Not sure he was white either. Forget the race card.

Further comments allow slurs on his character that suggest he is motivated by money (8 comments) or his perceived arrogance (15 comments) or lack of ability (6 comments). As Burdsey (2011a) has previously mentioned, Khan invokes discussions that are invariably less about the fight and more about his identity and character. Likewise the criticisms of his boxing ability seem to echo the biological stereotype of the 'weak Asian' body (Kilvington 2012). Interestingly Dirs notes that when other boxers or athletes lose fights, little is said about their non-sporting personas and few (if any) are questioned about loyalty (Dirs 2013).

The emergence of new media has opened up the sporting public sphere for comments that have little do with the sport but more with social prejudices that are a reflection of wider society. It is also clear that the utopian dream that cyberspace is a post race sanctuary is not the case. Just as access to the internet is dependent on economic and social factors that can be considered racialised, actions on the online forums/chat rooms/tweets reflect these inequalities.

Consider the following that were posted when Khan lost to Danny Garcia in the US in 2012 (see www.youtube.com/watch?v=pakesTezKYo)

like most muslims from england all mouth no chin skinny ass weak legs

hate that paki prick

Amir Khan should go back to working in a corner shop.

Those rag heads shouldnt be boxing! Hahahahaha

These overtly racist comments, supported by a combination of racial ideologies, show that cyberspace remains a challenging space. It could be suggested that unless racism and 'race' think is adequately tackled in 'offline' society – racism will remain a problem in online society – even when discussing the sporting arena. As Stuart Hall (1997: 3) notes, 'cultural meanings are not only "in the head". They organize and regulate social practices, influence our conduct and consequently have real, practical effects'.

Throughout Western Europe, Muslim communities from a variety of different ethnic backgrounds constitute the poorest strata in society (Fekete 2002). Various demographic researchers have shown that Muslims suffer poor housing, poor health and high levels of unemployment (Abbas 2007). However much they seek to identify themselves as British, young Muslims regularly find that others assume them to be first and foremost Muslim. A discourse has been produced which directly links European Muslims with support for terrorism, fundamentalism, 'illegal immigration' and Orientalist stereotypes (Saeed 2007). European Muslims are repeatedly asked by voices in the media and by politicians on all sides to make more strenuous efforts to integrate into Western society, and re-assert their loyalty to the nation states in a manner never asked of other non-Muslim groups (Saeed and Blain 1999). Identity is construed in rigid and exclusive terms and being seen to belong to 'the other' means being subject to the Orientalist gaze and pronounced backward or uncivilised. Furthermore it appears that 'racial discussion' in new media is not simply confined to political and social spheres. All aspects of popular culture that young Muslims attempt to engage in are treated with suspicion and hostility (Saeed 2014). Hence a strange dichotomy occurs – young Muslims are criticised as being insular and separatist, yet when they participate in wider culture they face hostility and suspicion.

The post 9/11 world has clearly seen an explosion of anti-Muslim racism and discrimination (Saeed 2007, 2011, 2014). What is evident is that this anti-Muslim racism can be traced back to colonial discussions of 'race'. Certainly recent work by Meer and Nayak (2013) note that the contemporary world is still troubled and clearly needs to understand the ideologies and histories of 'race' thinking and racism itself. When one considers the complexities of 'race' and ethnicity inside virtual worlds, the already difficult questions of what constitutes 'race' in real worlds are magnified.

## Conclusion

To understand the racist abuse that Amir Khan has faced online, various factors need to be considered. The relative anonymity that social media provides allows the possibility for explicit statements to be posted (whether they are firmly believed or not) knowing that justification for these comments will be rarely required on a personal or face-to-face basis. The nature of racist abuse Khan has received online takes two broad forms. First, he is the victim of biological racism that suggests that certain ethnic groups – namely South Asians – are physically weak and hence lack a 'natural' sporting ability. Second, he has suffered a cultural racism that implies Muslims are incompatible with the West and indeed pose a threat to secular multiculturalism.

Khan is depicted at times as 'the ideal Muslim', yet this representation does not take into account the racialised discourse that emerges online and in new media. One of the sad features of online racism is that despite this sphere being characterised as new media, the discussion of 'race' and racism could easily be considered as old fashioned or a return to biological racism. New media, old prejudices.

# 8  US sport, racism and social media

## Introduction

This chapter will examine social media racism with regards to the National Hockey League (NHL) and the National Basketball Association (NBA). It will explore the racial, ethnic and cultural stereotypes of African American players within the NHL and Asian American athletes within the NBA. Both these 'racial' groups are considered minorities within their respective sports and are arguably deemed 'outsiders'. Put simply, it may appear somewhat surprising to observe an Asian American slam dunk their team to victory in the NBA, especially when we consider that almost 82 per cent of its players are black (NBA Online 2009). Similarly, due to ice hockey's hegemonic whiteness, some fans may double take at the sight of African Americans skating out in the Eastern Conference.

The study will focus on two key athletes/events. First, we shall critically analyse the online abuse that Washington Capitals winger, Joel Ward, encountered after his series winning goal against the Boston Bruins in 2012. Second, we will investigate the online treatment of Jeremy Lin. Lin, who had previously been used sparingly by his former club New York, shot to fame in the summer of 2012 after leading his team to an impressive winning streak. His role in this feat caused widespread acclaim leading to 'affectionate' nicknames such as 'Linsanity', 'Lintastic', 'Lin Dynasty' and 'Super Lintendo', to name but a few.

But, before we can discuss racism and stereotyping on social media, it is important to first provide an overview of foreign migration to America in order to further comprehend and contextualise the comments that can be observed in the contemporary digital public sphere.

## African/Asian American migration and contemporary representations

The story of African Caribbean migration to America is perhaps more widely known in comparison to the migratory journeys of East Asian groups. Nevertheless, African Caribbean migrants, who are the most established 'foreign' group in the United States, are the product of the Atlantic slave trade and European colonialism. The first wave occurred in the early twentieth century as hundreds of black immigrants began to enter. Yet, by 1924, the numbers had risen sharply as over 12,000 black immigrants were admitted (Johnson 2008). In the following year, restrictions were enforced which limited the number of 'coloured' immigrants entering the United States.

Johnson (2008: 80) points out that Ira Reid, who was the first to publish a comprehensive account of black immigrant experiences, found that '31.4 percent had been industrial workers and 40.4 percent had been servants or laborers'. African Caribbean immigrants therefore have a long history within manual trades. These statistics correlate with the dominant images of the centuries before as black slaves were naturally regarded to be 'best suited' for physical, and not mental, tasks (Malik 1996: 62). The stereotype of the strong, fast and powerful African has therefore been manifest for centuries (Brookes 2002; Farrington *et al.* 2012; Hoberman 1997).

The second wave of Caribbean immigration began after the Second World War. But, this wave was short lived as severe restrictions were enforced by the McCarran-Walter Act in 1952. The third and final wave, which was influenced by the Civil Rights Movement, continued into the twenty-first century. Now, in contemporary America, it has been reported that white children under the age of five will soon be a minority group (Sherwell 2013).

On the other hand, the early 1700s saw the first Asian immigrants arrive in America, although it was not until the mid-nineteenth century until Asian groups descended on mass. During this time many arrived as labourers and worked for the California Gold Rush and on Hawaiian plantations. However, as Shek (2006: 381) indicates, by the early 1900s 'employment opportunities were ... limited in scope, consisting primarily of "feminine" work such as laundry, housekeeping, and cooking, which translated in restaurant work'. For Nakamura (2008), these jobs constructed and even solidified the 'feminized' representation of Asian Americans.

Throughout the 1900s, notions of gender and physical effeminacy began to dominate Asian American representations. Films, television, cartoons and Broadway shows stereotyped and ridiculed Asian American men, questioning their sexual orientations. Shek (2006: 381) comments that white actors regularly 'put on "yellow face"' and taped their eyes to resemble looking Chinese or Japanese. One of the more shocking and memorable moments of stereotyping can be observed in Mickey Rooney's performance of Mr Yuni-oshi in *Breakfast at Tiffany's*. Freeman (2012) argues that Mr Yunioshi 'gives the movie its true flavour. It's hard to call a film glamorous when it features a white actor playing an Asian stereotype that would put a Tintin cartoon to shame'. With regards to gender, Shek (2006: 381) adds that in the Broadway production of Madame Butterfly, 'the effeminate image of Asian American men became intertwined with issues of sexuality when the lead character was a cross-dressing Chinese spy who falls in love with a British male spy'.

Although Chinese immigration was specifically controlled during the late nineteenth century, the Immigration Act of 1965 paved the way for the second wave of Asian immigration. But this time, Asian groups did not enter as labourers, they entered as educated professionals. Arguably, this merely helped strengthen the stereotype that Asian males were averse to manual trades and more suited to restaurant or office work. Due to the rise of Asian professionals into the United States, 'the 1970s saw the emergence of the model minority myth, a stereotype that applied to all Asian Americans' (Shek 2006: 381). This 'model minority' myth indicates that Asian Americans work hard, contribute to the economy and integrate/assimilate without struggle. According to Nakamura (2008: 190), Asian Americans, akin to gay men, are represented as 'privileged consumers rather than workers or laborers', adding that they are commonly stereotyped as 'laundry-men or effeminate dandies' (Nakamura 2008: 186).

The 'Jack Nicklaus syndrome' is apparent here as it typifies the unconscious acceptance of racial difference (Hoberman 1997; Hylton 2009). Before Tiger Woods sedimented himself as one of the world's best golfers, Jack Nicklaus commented that African American golfers could not compete at the highest level because of their muscle structure (Hatfield 1996). Success and failure, or inclusion and exclusion, can therefore be explained as a 'race' thing (Kilvington 2012). After all, Jayaratne *et al.* (in Zarate 2009: 388) reported that 27 per cent of 600 interviewees believed that 'genetic influences accounted for some or most race differences across traits'.

St Louis (2004) discusses the inductivist theory of racial success. He argues that observations lead to generalised discourses which become common-sense assumptions. For example, if one observes a male and female in a sprinting event, without prejudice, it produces 'observation statements' (Chalmers 1982). If the male beats the female in the race, one could conclude that the individual male is the faster runner. Yet, this observation could lead to a generalisation: men are faster than women. As St Louis (2004: 36) postulates then, 'the inductivist approach recognizes the need to establish the necessary standards that allow a finite list of singular observation statements to be extrapolated into a general law'. Because African Americans are over represented in the NBA and National Football League (NFL), one could argue that they are simply 'naturally' better when compared with other 'racial' or ethnic groups. On the other hand, as the 'Jack Nicklaus syndrome' uncovered, when groups are excluded or under represented from certain sports, it could be argued that the group in question do not possess the physical or 'racial' requirements that are needed to succeed in that particular sport.

Jeremy Lin (Houston Rockets) has battled racio-cultural stereotypes en route to becoming a professional basketball star in the NBA. Willie O'Ree (Boston Bruins) and Kevin Weekes (Florida Panthers), among others, similarly have had to endure racial abuse on their journeys into the NHL. Although 'race' has been employed to explain and even justify the over and under representation of ethnic groups in sport (Farrington *et al.* 2012; Hylton 2009; Kilvington 2012), we must understand that 'race' is an invalid biological concept (Malik 1996; Miles 1989; Omi and Winant 1994).

For Cashmore (2005), upbringing and culture creates elite athletes, not 'race'. The closer one is to a field then, in this case sport, the more likely one is able to 'fit in'. Sporting minorities are therefore believed to lack the appropriate 'cultural passports' (Bauman 1988) and are thus denied the 'entry ticket' (Back *et al.* 2001: 141). One's inclusion and success within sport then arguably depends on one's cultural, social and economic capitals, as well as one's physique (Bourdieu 1984). But, importantly, we are always able to modify our habitus, it is never static (Webb *et al.* 2002). As a result, fields, meaning cultural practices, have changed and some sports have ethnically diversified.

In spite of these changes though, African American ice hockey players continue to face racism on and off the ice. It appears that such players are not accepted by some sections of the NHL fan base. For Asian American basketball players such as Lin, a flurry of stereotypes have followed in the media and on social media sites. The racism that we shall explore in this chapter will focus on 'racial' and cultural stereotypes, notions of belonging and exclusion.

## Joel Ward, the NHL and 'twacism'

Sports including football, athletics, boxing and even cricket have endured a long and unwanted association with racism. Overt racism, for instance, is still a major problem in football as Croatia, Russia and Spain were all fined by UEFA for their fans' racist abuse at the European Championships in 2012. Without surprise, a multitude of authors have thus critically analysed 'race' and racism in the sporting world (Back *et al.* 2001; Brookes 2002; Burdsey

2007; Cashmore 2005; Farrington *et al.* 2012; Hoberman 1997; Hylton 2009). With regards to ice hockey, 'race' and racism could be considered peripheral due to the sport's traditional mono-ethnicity or 'whiteness'.

However, for non-followers of the NHL, it might be surprising to hear that racism has been present for over half a century. There has been a steady influx of African American players since Willie O'Ree blazed a trial in the mid-1950s. Although O'Ree encountered some discrimination at Bruins, Toronto and Montreal, he faced greater hostility in Detroit, New York and Chicago. Tony McKegney, another African American pioneer of the late 1970s, played for 13 seasons but like O'Ree, he too faced racial abuse. In 1997, the NHL investigated the racism of Peter Worrell, of Florida Panthers, as Tampa Bay Lightning's players were alleged to have used racial slurs. In the same year, Worrell faced further discrimination as Craig Berube, of Washington Capitals, was suspended and fined over $7,000 for calling Worrell a 'monkey' (Russo 1997). In 2002, former Florida Panthers goaltender, Kevin Weekes, had a banana thrown at him while playing in Montreal. And, in 2011, Philadelphia Flyers winger Wayne Simmonds encountered a similar experience as a banana landed in his path during a penalty shootout defeat against Detroit Red Wings. This led Simmonds to comment: 'I guess it's something I obviously have to deal with – being a black player playing a predominantly white sport' (ESPN Online 2011). Similarly with other sports, the NHL is not exempt from racism. And, as we shall witness, with the advent of social media, it could be argued that racism has found yet another platform to thrive.

This case study will focus on the racism that Joel Ward, of the Washington Capitals, faced on Twitter following his overtime series-winner against the Boston Bruins in April 2012. With only moments to play, Ward, a Canadian whose parents were from Barbados, slapped in the rebound to eliminate the defending champions from the Stanley Cup. Ward's goal was not only the most important one of his career, but, for Anson Carter, a former Bruins and Capitals winger, also of Barbadian descent, it marked 'one of the biggest NHL moments ever for a black player' (in Mail Online 2012). Unfortunately, this momentous and euphoric occasion turned sour as, within minutes, Joel Ward was the subject of social media abuse. For some viewers, and Bruins fans, they did not observe a Capital, an unlucky rebound or the unpredictability of the playoffs, they observed nothing more than a black man. The following tweets demonstrate the hostility towards 'blackness' in the league:

Joe Daaboul @JoeDaaboul
Ward you fucking nigger

Zack Flesher @Flesher91
So … The nigger scores the game winner? **#shitty**

Devin @GeraldHart635
Of all people to score it had to be the Nigger…

Jessi Lauren @rawrimdinoJessi
FUCKJNG NIGGER! **#bruins**

Brandon Gaucher @Gaucherhockey24
Bruins lost to a dumb cotton picking purple dicked Nigger!!!! **#CHOICE!!!!!**

@Grizzlymarshall
Fucking stupid arrogant, smelly, useless, waste of life, sad excuse for a NHL hockey playing NIGGER!!!!

CotyShean @cboogie20
FUCKING LYNCH THE NIGGER **#justthatonethough**

@EthandaGXD
that nigger deserves to hang.

Being the 'lone-wolf' in a mono-ethnic environment enhances one's chances of being raced and marked 'Other'. Tweeters who posted racial epithets, seen above, did not see past Ward's raced body (Farrington *et al.* 2012; Kilvington 2012). The 'Other' is black, positioned on the periphery, whereas whites command the centre through processes that 'normalise' 'whiteness'. As Hylton (2009: 66) adds, 'The discursive power that is embodied through the "discourse of othering" (Riggins 1997) causes whiteness to be "inside", "included", "powerful", the "we", the "us", the "answer" as opposed to the problem, and most important of all, unspoken'.

It has been suggested that blatant/overt racism, or 'racial microaggressions', are just 'part of the game' (Burdsey 2011a, 2011b; Long and Hylton 2002). The 'rationalization of racial abuse' is therefore 'legitimized on the grounds that other players are abused because they are short, fat, bald or old: "That's how people express themselves when they get emotional"' (Long *et al.* 1997: 257). Hence, 'the denial of racism is itself a product of the normalisation of racist attitudes, the inevitable outcome is its continued reproduction' (ibid.: 256–257).

As Rowe (2004) postulates, racism can sometimes slip out during dramatic events, and, for Fiske (2010: 8), this constitutes a 'knee jerk' reaction.

As Bodenhausen *et al.* (2009) state, we are more likely to avoid racism when we have time to consider our response. Because prejudice, stereotypic thinking and discrimination can occur instantaneously, it leads to the 'heat of the moment' defence (Long and Hylton 2002; Rowe 2004). This popular defence can be observed in the backtracking words of @Spee_Durr following his racial abuse of Joel Ward:

> I apologize for my last tweet dropping the 'n-bomb' and for anyone I may have offended.

> I'm not a racist, just the heat of the moment.

Because Ward scored a dramatic winner to knock out the Bruins then, can Bruins fans be afforded some sympathy as their tweets were posted 'in the moment'? In a word, no, this language is unacceptable off and online. However, this racism highlights the broader social factors in the disposition towards 'race' and racism.

Feagin (2010) suggests that perpetrators of racism tend to commit such acts in spaces where they believe the subjects of their racial discrimination are unlikely to be. The ethnic breakdown of Twitter users in America, however, reveals that 25 per cent of online African Americans now use Twitter, compared with 9 per cent of whites (Smith 2011). Nonetheless, 'Caucasians' still dominate the American 'Twitter-sphere' at 67 per cent, in comparison to 17 per cent of African Americans and 12 per cent of Hispanics (Quantcast Online 2013). In turn, Twitter is perhaps regarded by some whites to be a somewhat closed and private space. Feagin (2010) labels this the 'backstage'. Hylton (2013: 14) adds, 'Through the seeming privacy of the Internet, its individualistic communications process and the relative anonymity of the interactants, cyberspace becomes a "safe space" for normally borderline and more abhorrent views'.

Ward reflected on the incident by providing his experiences of racism during his career: 'Growing up, at a few minor tournaments, you catch a few kids saying things ... But (at this level) I've never heard anything. I know other guys have, I believe, but I've had nothing directed to me like that' (in Allen 2012). As Kilvington and Price (2013) note, racisms are more prevalent at the lower echelons of sport as these structures tend to be less regulated, have less authoritarian figures (referees, assistants, stewards, etc.) and are positioned away from television cameras and sound recording devices. Therefore, although Ward encountered some racism at minor tournaments, it is not surprising that it decreased as he progressed up the ice hockey ladder. But, by Ward's own admission, he has never faced racial abuse to the degree that he did online. In light of this, one could argue that it is extremely surprising that social factors such as 'race' have been given little attention in the cyber culture literature (Hylton 2013; Silver 2000).

It could be suggested that some white social network users feel liberated or even invincible as they are free to voice their opinions in online spaces anonymously or under aliases without fear of being caught or prosecuted. Despite a 'report abuse' button being introduced by Twitter in August 2013, racism, sexism, homophobia, trolling, etc. still continues. The success of this positive addition remains to be seen. Hence, those who post racist tweets operate in, what they believe, is a 'safe space' (Hylton 2013: 14) in the 'backstage' arena (Feagin 2010).

Not only was Ward mindlessly brandished with the 'n-word' on Twitter, he faced further abuse as racial and cultural stereotypes were resonant in some posts. For example, notions of 'whiteness', 'race', identity, belonging and exclusion are just some of the themes that can be observed in the tweets below:

> Jeffery Crispo @CrispoCream
> **#bruins** just got beat by a nigger I thought hockey was a white mans game **#wtf** fuck ward
>
> Zack Vanasse @zvanasse30
> stupid nigger go play basketball hockey is a white sport
>
> @2_thirty_3
> Fuck noooo **#bruins #fuck #nigger** nigger u suck your black go play b ball
>
> @lake617
> Fuck nigger scored **#go2thenba**

For these tweeters, the NHL is perceived to be racially exclusive; it is not welcome to 'outsiders'. Instead, Ward should go play *his* sport, basketball, simply because of his 'blackness'. Because the NHL is considered the 'whitest' of the four major American sports, some fans perceive it as 'theirs', as 'pure', as 'white'. As Burdsey (2011a: 13) postulates, then, '*cultural* attributes', as well as 'race', are also 'employed in the process of "Othering" particular groups'. As some tweets suggest, it is not culturally acceptable for Ward to compete in the 'white man's' game.

Bourdieu's (1984) notion of the habitus becomes relevant within this discussion. Webb *et al.* (2002: xii) define the habitus as 'the way in which individuals "become themselves" – develop attitudes and dispositions – and, on the other hand, the ways in which those individuals engage in practices'.

Bourdieu (1977: 81) states that one's habitus is 'laid down in each agent by his earliest upbringing' and our habitus thus leads to group or 'collective mobilization'. In short, our habitus, 'the unifying, generative principle of all practices', positions us into social groups (Bourdieu 1984: 173). For Said (1985: 45), men are divided into two groups, ' "us" (Westerners) and "they" (Orientals)', or, in the context of this analysis: 'Us' (white) versus 'they' (black). In simple terms, both social groups represent binary opposites.

We could allude to Cohen's (1996) research of racial 'no-go' areas here as he comments that 'race' becomes a marker of territory (Alexander and Knowles 2005). Said (1985: 54) argues that designating a 'familiar space' which 'is "ours" and an unfamiliar space beyond "ours" which is "theirs" is a way of making geographical distinctions'. These 'geographic boundaries' are thus split along 'social, ethnic and cultural' lines (ibid.). For some fans, ice hockey represents a racial 'no-go' area for African Americans. The NFL, NBA and Major League Baseball (MLB) have all ethnically diversified but, for the NHL, it is still largely white, and it appears that some fans fear diversification and thus want to protect this 'white' space. It is not a 'geographic boundary' that we observe, in a literal sense, but a sporting one.

Kevin Weekes, who currently provides match analysis on *Hockey Night in Canada*, displayed his sadness towards the abuse of Ward. He tweeted: '@NHL @hockeynight Utterly disgusted/disheartened by racist comments by so-called **#Fans** towards my friend **#JoelWard** for scoring a goal…'. Weekes sympathised with the Capitals winger as he too has been subjected to racism on social media. He notes that 'some "despicable" losers' have used the 'n-word' to describe him (in Zeisberger 2012). He adds,

> There are some Saturdays when I'm doing Hockey Night or we're doing our (After Hours) interview segment and I check Twitter to find stuff [racism] … I'll get (garbage) like 'What are you doing covering hockey? You should be covering basketball'.
>
> (Zeisberger 2012)

Although black players have been competing in the NHL for over half a century, Simmonds, Weekes and Ward, among others, still face resistance and rejection by some sections of the NHL fan base. Some hashtags emphasised that ice hockey, and America generally, should remain white as Twitter user, @mastabates23 posted **#gobacktothejungle**, while @Khall1013 tweeted **#gobacktoafrica**.

Essentialist discourses of 'race' can also be observed in some posts. Although black athletes are commonly described as 'natural' (Brookes 2002; Hoberman 1997; Hylton 2009; Farrington *et al.* 2012), notably in sports that require speed and strength, some tweets displayed surprise at seeing a black player not only score, but show skating prowess. Because African American players are still largely under-represented in ice hockey, they have been less successful in combating ability related stereotypes. Despite nurture playing a major role in one's sporting successes (Cashmore 2005; Coyle 2010), the comments below indicate that black players are simply not as gifted as whites on the ice.

@mikeanzideo
Haha that nigger actually did something

@BradenAxtman
Did a nigger just score the game winner in game 7 **#diddntknowthey couldskate**

Both tweets indicate surprise and confusion. For @BardenAxtman, Ward's goal appears a revelation as he/she now understands that 'black' people, in the most homogenised sense imaginable, can skate, i.e. play ice hockey. Tweeter, @jrharding96, also demonstrates shock, noting: 'I'm still confused how a nigger just scored on tim Thomas'. According to the author of this post, Thomas, the Bruins goaltender, who has 15 years league experience, should not be beaten by a black player. For @Begos_8, Thomas's crime is a little more serious as he/she comments, 'Joel Ward your a nigger. Holtby, get a life. I never wanna see Tim Thomas in a bruins jersey ever again **#washedup #bum**'. Thus, according to @Begos_8, Thomas, who merely conceded a goal, deserves to be sacked because Ward just so happens to have two parents that were born in Barbados.

There have been numerous examples of overt racism on the ice in the last decade. Yet, these incidents remain isolated, and, when they do occur, they tend to be the actions of individuals or relatively small groups. Arguably, then, the Joel Ward incident marks a new chapter in the complex interplay between 'race' and racism in the NHL. It could be argued that this incident represents the most severe case of racism ever witnessed in the sport. The quantity of comments, the content of them, and the terminology used strongly indicates that racism is not declining. Hundreds, if not thousands, of racist tweets were posted. But, if those tweeters were not sitting safely behind their keyboard, would they have shouted the same words from the stands? Our response would be, no, on the whole, they would not. As this section has indicated, online comments are perceived to be deposited in a 'safe space' (Hylton 2013), a space that reflects a 'white privileged' environment (Dyer 1997; Hylton 2009; Long *et al.* 1997; Long and Hylton 2002) and one where it can be done 'backstage' (Feagin 2010), away from the eyes of 'Others'.

That said, sometimes, racist tweeters can be caught out. Students attending the high schools of Gloucester and Denver (Massachusetts), the Cumberland, R.I., School District and Franklin Pierce University in North Hampshire, who were alleged to have used racial epithets towards Ward, were placed under investigation. And, following a probe, five students at Gloucester High School were suspended from athletic programmes and forced to forfeit any leadership roles in extracurricular activities. First of all, these offenders arguably got off lightly, in comparison to others who have been found guilty of social media racism in other countries. Second, because only a very small number of people faced any ramifications, it further emphasises that the overwhelming majority of racist tweeters escape undetected. And, third, because only high school students were investigated, it highlights that adults, or those outside the education system, are given a free pass. No person was arrested for the racial abuse of Joel Ward. This is hardly surprising as, within the United States, there has been little debate, development and legal discussion over cyber racism. Until this is addressed, it is likely that social media racism will continue.

## 'Linsanity', the NBA and social media racism

Los Angeles born Jeremy Lin, whose parents emigrated from Taiwan, is the only active Asian American player in the NBA. Point-Guard Lin announced himself in 2012 after scoring a combined total of 51 points in his first two games for the Knicks before adding a career-high of 38 in a narrow victory over Kobe Bryant and the Los Angeles Lakers. His impressive performances captivated audiences worldwide, leading to a global frenzy known as 'Linsanity'. Lin, who also studied economics at Harvard University, has become the most successful and high profile Asian American in NBA history. To date, there has only ever been five Asian Americans that have competed in the NBA. Wataru Misaka, who was the NBA's first Asian American and first non-Caucasian player, Raymond Townsend, Corey Gaines and Rex Walters complete the list.

The 'panethnic' nature of the homogenising term, Asian American, must be addressed at this juncture. Misaka and Walters are ethnically described as Japanese American, Townsend is categorised as Filipino American, Gaines could be described as African/Japanese American while Lin would be more accurately labelled Taiwanese American. Lin is also the first Asian American player in NBA history to have two Asian parents. These players, despite their different upbringings, cultures, traditions and languages, are grouped under the same racialised term that, according to Omi (1996), was purposefully employed following the civil rights movement in order to form a larger political constituency. This shared racial or 'panethnic' grouping appears to eclipse other identity markers such as nationality. Nakamura (2008: 75) notes that the

> emphasis on racial or visible phenotypic difference as the primary defining quality of all nonwhite people has always been an especially salient aspect of America's war with Asian nations and resulted in what was called in Vietnam the 'mere gook rule', by which any dead Vietnamese was counted as a dead enemy ... This elision of cultural differences between different groups from Asia produces misrecognitions that often anger Asian Americans; one of these manifestations is the cliché 'they all look the same'.

Using Jeremy Lin as a focal point, it allows us to address some of the key issues that affect wider contemporary Asian American communities. Cultural racism, questions of identity, constructions of gender and racial micro-aggressions are just some of the themes that will be critically explored in both a media and social media context.

The first example of racism that we shall refer to is arguably the most famous. Following Jeremy's 'Lin-tastic' display in a victory over the Dallas Mavericks in February 2012, ESPN published a story with the headline 'Chink in the Armour' (De John and Kennedy 2012). Unsurprisingly, the headline, which appeared on ESPN's mobile website, was removed within 35 minutes of being posted due to its racially offensive content. In the aftermath, Anthony Federico, who was responsible for writing the headline, was fired. In addition, sports anchor Max Breto was suspended for 30 days after he had used the same phrase live on air.

It is interesting to note how Lin responded to one tweeter who brandished him, quite simply, a 'chink'. Lin not only re-tweeted the message but offered the love of Jesus to the offender behind the racial slur. Lin said: 'This is happening in 2012? Jesus loves you bro and I do too'. This calm response arguably adds to the 'model minority' myth.

These incidents, and the nonchalant way in which the word 'chink' was used, illustrates that, for some, America is, or is fast becoming, colour-blind. Colour-blindness thus refers to a utopian vision of society, one where people are considered socially, economically and politically equal as 'race' and ethnicity no longer transmit any disadvantages or advantages. For Hylton (2009: 32), it is a device which 'maintains dominant hegemonies and social hierarchies by regularly ignoring discriminatory factors'. In short, the headline emphasises its belief in a 'post-race' world as racism has become a 'thing of the past' (Burdsey 2011b: 261). Racist terminology becomes 'post-racist' from a white privilege perspective.

ESPN sportswriter Jason Whitlock's tweet further adds to the perception of a colour-blind society as he joked that 'Some lucky lady in NYC is gonna feel a couple inches of pain tonight' after Lin scored 38 points against the Lakers. Not only is this comment racist, it is also highly misogynistic. For Whitlock then, it appears to be perfectly acceptable to invoke emasculating racial stereotypes about Asian males having undersized genitalia. Despite a public apology, this example once again demonstrates that it is acceptable to racialise or racially stereotype Asian American communities. What would the public reaction have been if Whitlock, or any other journalist, used a similar analogy for a black player?

For Rowe (2004), Boyle and Haynes (2000), and Bernstein and Blain (2003), sports commentators such as Whitlock hold powerful positions as they are able to influence our understandings on contentious issues. It could be argued that Whitlock's tweet authorises this type of racist behaviour. Similar comments to Whitlock's can be found on twitter.

Tucker Max @TuckerMax                                   10 Feb 12
Whatever girl in NYC gets to have sex with Jeremy Lin tonight is very lucky, even if she cant actually feel it

Evil Sports @EvilAnnouncer                                  18 Dec
I have a challenge for my followers. Winner will get announced. How small is Jeremy Lin's Chinese dick. **#EvilChallenge**

Juan McCain @BorderCoyote                                27 Feb 12
Just had sex with Jeremy Lin, or maybe Jackie Chan, or maybe just some random Asian guy. Point is, my penis is fucking huge by comparison.

For Tucker Max, his tweet reiterates Whitlock's poor attempt at a joke. Evil Sports, which is arguably trying to be ironic considering its name, not only utilises biological stereotypes, but it shows ignorance towards Lin's heritage as it falsely labels him 'Chinese'. Moreover, this tweet omits the word 'American' from the beginning, indicating that Lin's 'race' is not only fixed, but it is the primary marker of his 'Other' identity. Juan McCain's 'joke' is also rooted in the idea of racial difference. According to McCain, not only do Asians have small penises, they 'all look the same' (Nakamura 2008: 75). For Sue *et al.* (2007: 273), these comments are examples of 'racial microaggressions' which are 'brief, everyday exchanges that send denigrating messages to people of color because they belong to a racial minority group'. Some individuals, notably those who believe in a 'post-race' world, perceive these 'racial microaggressions' or 'microinsults' (Sue *et al.* 2007) to be just 'banter' and nothing more.

Because Asian Americans are considered the 'model minority', one could suggest that they are perceived, by some, to have escaped racism. In turn, anti-Asian discriminatory terms such as chink are considered more socially acceptable than anti-black terms like nigger. Lin's journey, inside and outside sport, symbolises the American dream as anyone can succeed regardless of their 'race', ethnicity, religion, gender, etc. A professional basketball player, a Harvard graduate and now part of the elite or upper classes, Lin reflects the egalitarianism of contemporary America. This success story even led one Asian American ESPN columnist, Jay Caspian Kang (in Zirin 2012), to write: 'If you can't look at Jeremy Lin and see why America is the greatest country in the world, well, then you don't understand America'.

Yet, however true or appealing this may sound, this mythical vision of society is artificial as Asian Americans, as well as other minority groups, still encounter ignorance, discrimination and stereotyping. Despite Asian American's 'model minority' status, we must understand that a

> move up the social ladder does not mean a move towards a greater sense of racial equality … [in short] although some sports stars have an elevated social status, it does not make them impervious to any form of racism.
>
> (Farrington *et al.* 2012: 149)

We have observed that Lin, like many other sports stars who are minorities in their field, is represented as Asian first, and basketball star second (Farrington *et al.* 2012). In the process, racial and cultural stereotypes are regularly attached to Lin. The most notable example of cultural stereotyping comes from Ben & Jerry's ice cream flavour, 'Taste the Lin-Sanity' which originally featured vanilla frozen yoghurt, lychee honey swirls and fortune-cookie pieces. This new flavour sparked outrage as it not only essentialises Asian American groups, it reinforces stereotypes and blatantly marks Lin out as 'Other', as different, a player on the periphery, an outsider. In addition, following a Knicks victory against the Sacramento Kings, the Madison Square Garden (MSG) Network aired a TV graphic that superimposed Lin's head above a fortune cookie which included the caption, 'The Knicks Good Fortune'. Cultural stereotyping can also be witnessed online as YouTube user, 'WDecayed', 'bets' that Lin is paid 'with Noodles and chicken wings [at] the end of each match'.

Twitter and YouTube comments were critically examined for this case study and various themes/codes were generated. On Twitter, over-hyping and Harvard appeared to be the most prominent discussion topics while on YouTube, over-hyping, 'race' and cultural stereotyping dominated the posts. The following tweets emphasise the fascination with Lin's Harvard background and his somewhat superior intelligence:

@KGTrashTalk @KGTrashTalk                                    27 Apr
Jeremy Lin over there on the bench doing math problems in his head.


jeff green fan @JeffTeamgreen                                27 Apr
@KGTrashTalk lol he fixed my computer with his eyes closed too


B @Yo_MrWhite                                              3 May 12
Jeremy Lin looks like the Knick's accountant sitting over there on the
bench


Coach Spo @SpoLogic                                        16 Jul 12
Stephen A says the Knicks should let Jeremy Lin walk. Must be so hard
to let go of your accountant/point guard


Not Stan Van Gundy @StanVanGundyNot                          5 Jul 12
The **#Rockets** are Linsane to give Jeremy Lin that kind of money. Now
if they need an accountant, that's a different story


pat … @thatpatp                                            12 Feb 12
Jeremy Lin's parents still probably disappointed that he didn't end up
being an accountant or a physicist. **#ChinkBalla88**


IP @TheIPnYc                                                4 Feb 12
Jeremy Lin is trending! Nothing like a guy who looks like an accountant
dominating at an NBA game **#jealous**


Ted Black @teddy_ballgame36                                   Feb 12
If someone showed me a pic of Jeremy Lin & asked me what his pro-
fession was i'd never guess Knicks starting PG **#accountant?**
**#mathteacher?**


For Hylton (2009: 14), cultural racism is often 'difficult to detect and
much easier to deny'. Thus, for some of the above tweets, the racism invoked
is very subtle and can easily be overlooked. Because Lin has a degree from
one of the most prestigious university's in America, he is clearly a very intel-
ligent and hard working individual. Therefore, he could literally be an
accountant or a maths teacher. Some would argue that these comments
display banter, humour and must not be taken seriously. On the other hand,
once we have theoretically grounded these statements and have contextual-
ised them historically as well as contemporaneously, we are able to comprehend their racist nature.

First, we need to revisit dominant representations of the Asian body in relation to sport. Bourdieu (1984: 217–218) posits that a sport is more likely to be embraced by 'a social class if it does not contradict that class's relation to the body'. This hypothesis can also be linked with the process of racialisation as the Occident's notion of the Asian body is one that lacks the necessary qualities needed to succeed in physically demanding sports, such as basketball (Said 1985). Hence, the Asian 'identity' becomes racialised as characteristics are unfairly ascribed to them (Back *et al.* 2001). Lin's raced body therefore contradicts dominant representations of 'Asianness' and this appears confusing for some basketball fans, such as @teddy_ballgame36.

Alexander and Knowles (2005) state that studying is considered to be a feminine pursuit while Hoberman (1997) adds that peer pressure steers African American students towards sport and away from education as academic excellence is equated with effeminacy and 'whiteness'. For Asian Americans, however, they are deemed to avoid manual professions and contact sports in favour of 'feminine' jobs or further education (Nakamura 2008; Shek 2006). This long serving stereotype, which has been reinforced by media images, has resulted in the Asian American man being positioned 'within the discourse of the contemporary dandy or metrosexual at best, outright queer at worst' (Nakamura 2008: 190). Hence, Lin 'looks like' an accountant or a maths teacher, not a basketball player, because his racialised body is not masculine enough to compete against superior, more athletically gifted and culturally suited 'races'.

There has also been much online debate over whether the nickname, 'the yellow mamba' is racist or not. The following YouTube comments highlight its popularity:

TheDjKrazybeats
The yellow mamba! LOOOOOOOOOOOOOOOOOOOOOOOOOOL

Freddi Fish
the yellow mamba XD

DAniel varkey
Haha XD YELLOW MAMBA!!!!!

SpasmedChicken
Pahahaha. 'The Yellow Mamba'.

shoryukenpower
lol the yellow mamba

During the Knicks versus Lakers game, in which Lin scored 38 points, ESPN aired an image of a fan holding up a sign that read, 'The Yellow Mamba'. Within minutes, this new nickname had gone viral and was being used across social network sites. But, to what extent is this nickname racist?

LA Lakers star, Kobe Bryant, reportedly anointed himself the 'black mamba'. Therefore, one could argue that it is perfectly acceptable for Lin, because of his Taiwanese heritage, to assume the role of the 'yellow mamba'. However, there are multiple reasons why this nickname should be avoided. First, Bryant apparently gave himself the nickname 'black mamba' while Lin had 'yellow mamba' forced upon him. Second, a 'black mamba' is a type of snake and therefore this term has a double meaning as it also describes Bryant's speed and ability to weave or wriggle through tight defences. Conversely, there is no such creature as a 'yellow mamba'. Third, while some, or most, African Americans would identify themselves as being black, it is highly unlikely that Lin, or other Asian Americans, or Asians, would refer to themselves as being 'yellow'. Asian American is already a contested term, 'yellow', on the other hand, is even more problematic.

Despite this, the reactions and attitudes of the YouTube users above demonstrates their ignorance towards this racial term as 'lol' (laughs out loud) and 'haha' is employed. But, for the three tweeters below, they understand that this nickname is racist and yet, they still appear to find it humorous.

> Rasheed Kennedy @RasheedKennedy
> Y'all Wrong As Hell For Calling Jeremy Lin The 'Yellow Mamba' Lmao...

> David Ravitz @D_Ravitz
> Hahahahahahaha I just saw a sign that said 'The YELLOW Mamba' for Jeremy Lin! Racism at it's finest lol

> Drew Franklin @DrewFranklinKSR
> Calling Jeremy Lin 'Yellow Mamba' is racist. It's 'Yerro Mamba'.
> **#linsanity**

For Rasheed Kennedy, he states that it is 'wrong' to label Lin the 'yellow mamba' but then adds 'lmao' (laugh my ass off) to display his lack of offence. David Ravitz, on the other hand, indicates that the nickname is either racist, or, it should be celebrated as a fine example of racism. We would argue that the former is intended, but like the previous example, he too adds 'lol'. Finally, Drew Franklin successfully points out that the nickname is racist but then exacerbates the initial racialised term by adding

'Yerro Mamba' to imitate stereotypical constructions of 'Asian speech' patterns made popular in recent times by cultural texts such as *Team America* and *The Hangover* films. These comments demonstrate that anti-Asian racism tends to be decoded as humorous rather than offensive.

Although it can be difficult at times to know the real identity of online users, such as the tweeters above, D'Andrea and Daniels (1999: 97) postulate that for some whites, they refrain from discussing racism because they feel they will not be taken 'seriously' or they will 'be met with defensive reactions by many White people' they know. By adding 'lol', 'haha' or 'lmao' at the end of posts which condemn racism indicates that, for some social media users, they do not want to appear too politically correct.

That said, online anti-black racism almost always receives a fierce backlash. The anger and intensity that followed the online abuse of Joel Ward was impressive to observe. However, with regards to anti-Asian racism, there appears to be some confusion over what is and what is not racist. Vera and Feagin's (2004) work on what constitutes a racist event is noteworthy here. Of the seven identified themes, some fit with the online treatment of Jeremy Lin. First, there is white, or non-Asian, perpetrators. Second, the victim is Asian American. Third, the online discrimination ritualises racialised acts of attributing and denigrating 'Asianness'. Fourth, the media and social media examples included in this chapter reinforce perceptions of racial stratification and racial hierarchies in basketball. In short, it is evident that the social media examples incorporated in this chapter theoretically equate with racist events.

This case study has demonstrated that the notion of colour-blindness has obscured the societal view for many media writers and social media users. As we have shown, Lin has endured emasculating biological stereotypes, he has been raced as 'yellow' and he has faced varying degrees of cultural racism. Wesley Yang attempts to point out why Asian Americans are so heavily stereotyped in contemporary America. She notes that to be an Asian American means being not just part of a 'barely distinguishable' mass of 'people who are good at math and play the violin, but a mass of stifled, repressed, abused, conformist quasi-robots who simply do not matter, socially or culturally' (in Freeman 2012). The examples provided in this chapter illustrate that Asian Americans are still considered to be one dimensional, walking talking stereotypes that have had little opportunity to combat dominant media representations. Lin has the opportunity to enlighten mindsets and change people's perceptions of what it is to be Asian and American – he is, unfortunately, then, under an immense amount of pressure. Yet, with greater education and further cultural awareness, it is hoped that racism towards Asian Americans will decline, both on and offline.

# Conclusion

This chapter has explored concepts such as racisms, colour-blindness, exclusion, identities and 'whiteness' within an NHL and NBA context. The critical analysis of Joel Ward highlighted that 'automatic prejudice' is manifest as he was racially abused within minutes of scoring the winning goal (Bodenhausen *et al.* 2009). Twitter users also questioned Ward's belonging as his 'blackness' constitutes a paradox. The online racism that Ward encountered is arguably the most extreme example of racism ever witnessed in the NHL. Overt racism, of this magnitude, is no longer heard within the NHL stands. But, as Feagin (2010) suggests, social media allows users to deposit racist discourse covertly in the 'backstage' arena. As scholars of 'race' and racism, our attention should now turn to this new digital space as it continues to breathe life into an outdated, hierarchically obsessed imperial invention.

The case study of 'Linsanity' demonstrated that media writers and social media users have committed acts of instant stereotyping (Dovidio *et al.* 1986; Zarate 2009), which are commonly justified under the banter umbrella. Although anti-black racism is vehemently attacked, anti-Asian racism is arguably not met with the same ferocity. As a result, the boundary between anti-Asian racism and non-racism appears blurred. If society continues to believe in colour-blindness, a 'tolerance zone' will be upheld in which 'certain forms of racism are trivialized or ignored, and particular epithets or actions are exonerated' (Burdsey 2011b: 278). Because of this fallacy, Lin has been labelled 'chink', 'the yellow mamba', his head has appeared superimposed on fortune cookies and his being has been racialised and culturally stereotyped. In order to prevent further racial stereotyping of Lin, and future Asian American players, constructions of 'Asianness' need to be destabilised. With greater media exposure, it is believed that Asian American stereotypes will become less socially acceptable and will ultimately decline.

In sum, more action can be taken by the NHL and NBA in order to challenge social media racism. Although the Bruins and the Capitals responded immediately to condemn the racial abuse of Ward, the NHL appeared to lack urgency as they issued several brief statements the following day. 'The racially charged comments distributed via digital media following last night's game were ignorant and unacceptable. The people responsible for these comments have no place associating themselves with our game', read the official NHL statement. When racism does occur, the governing bodies must set the precedent and thus, both the NHL and NBA must act quickly, strongly and clearly against racism, on and offline. Perhaps harsher punishments for those found guilty of social media racism may act as a more successful deterrent. And, finally, although some NHL and NBA clubs have begun to educate their players on the role and importance of social media, the governing bodies could step in to facilitate the process and ensure that all players at all clubs receive training and guidance on social media.

# 9 The way forward

## Explanations and recommendations

### Introduction

This final chapter draws together the key messages from previous chapters to present explanations for sport related racism on social media – and the best ways to tackle the problem. It begins by critically examining the various factors likely to increase expressions of racism on social media. Once we are able to comprehend these causes, then it allows us to propose recommendations for reform. Therefore, the second half of the chapter will highlight a number of ways in which racism on social network sites can be controlled and reduced. We are under no illusion, however, that a perfect solution or 'quick-fix' exists. Hence, we will raise multiple ideas but will discuss them in a critical manner as we understand that each recommendation potentially harbours flaws. What we can agree on, though, is this, hate speech on social media represents a clear problem and one that deserves serious attention from the likes of social network sites, the Government and the legal system.

### Explanations

The purpose of this section is to highlight and discuss factors that are believed to increase and encourage the likelihood of racism on social network sites. Why has social media become such a breeding ground for racist content and abuse? Chapter four examined wider causes of racism in society by drawing on ideas from the field of social psychology. It also discussed previous research about racism on the internet. The following section develops these ideas, bringing in findings from our case studies, to focus on explanations specific to sport, racism and social media.

### Social context

If those found guilty of espousing racial hatred on social media receive weak penalties, such as an account being suspended or being banned from the site in question, it is unlikely that we will see a decrease in such behaviour. Social media users, and 'keyboard warriors' especially, often have multiple accounts and if one account is suspended or deleted due to a policy infringement, the user can simply opt for another account. However, if social network sites collectively incorporate stronger penalties for hate speech, this may help reduce social media racism. Bodenhausen *et al.* (2009) suggest that we rein in our prejudices due to societal penalties. We therefore conform to 'robust forms of egalitarianism that have come to dominate many contemporary societies' (ibid.: 115). Plant and Devine (in Bodenhausen *et al.* 2009) label this as an 'external motivation' to control prejudice as we tend not to articulate racist discourse because of our situational vulnerability. But, if hate speech goes unchallenged on social media sites, one may feel situationally protected.

### Nature of communication

The nature of communication is a fundamental difference between physical and online racism. For Crandall and Eshleman (2003: 424), anonymity 'is an important ingredient in prejudice-based aggression'. The following interviewee, who is an expert in criminology and hate-crime, notes that:

> Social media has given it [racism] a new forum; a new possibility for someone to lash out. What it does, though, is it puts the perpetrator in a position of relative safety; a position that they wouldn't enjoy in the physical world. In the physical world when people are lashing out, there will be a barely conscious calculation about the risk of doing that. Is the person going to retaliate to them? Is there a risk? So, on social media, that kind of risk is removed altogether, isn't it?
>
> (Interview 22 October 2013)

This comment indicates that social media provides offenders and potential offenders a 'safe space'; physically distant from the victim. Explicit forms of racism can be expressed without the fear of retaliation. Suler's discussion of 'invisibility' is therefore significant.

> This invisibility gives people the courage to go places and do things that they otherwise wouldn't ... Even with everyone's identity known, the opportunity to be physically invisible amplifies the disinhibition effect.

People don't have to worry about how they look or sound when they type a message. They don't have to worry about how others look or sound in response to what they say. Seeing a frown, a shaking head, a sigh, a bored expression, and many other subtle and not so subtle signs of disapproval or indifference can inhibit what people are willing to express.

(Suler 2004: 322)

As Suler adds, we are more likely to divulge personal information or our inner thoughts when we avoid eye contact, as this inhibits people. Psycho-analysts sit behind patients 'in order to remain a physically ambiguous figure, revealing no body language or facial expression, so that the patient has free range to discuss whatever he or she wants without feeling inhibited by how the analyst is physically reacting' (Suler 2004: 322). The nature of communication via social media allows users 'a built-in opportunity to' constantly 'keep one's eyes averted' (ibid.).

Another cause of social media racism is the quick and instantaneous nature of communication. Dr Jeni Kubota states that 'Information is transmitted in a rapid and unfiltered manner, and this allows for implicit racial bias to surface' (Interview 4 October 2013). In all of our case studies there are examples of social media users expressing prejudice and then, on reflection, seeking to distance themselves or backtrack from their earlier comments. The sheer speed of interaction on social media, one of its many appeals, means racism is more likely to occur.

In addition, if we possess a lack of personal information about the recipient and have had little prior contact with them, this will increase the possibility of hate speech online. In other words, if a user has had minimal or no social contact, both on and offline, with ethnic groups aside from their own, they may stereotype, and possess and express prejudicial views. Stangor (2009) argues that we are more prone to use stereotypes when we have had very little contact with the recipient or group. As social media transcends time, place and space, we are thus able to engage in dialogue with cyber-strangers who we may never meet in the physical world. For a potential offender then, if they do not know the victim and believe they will never cross paths, this aids the feeling of disinhibition. Moreover, they will be less likely to empathise with and relate to the recipient. As a result, this increases the possibility of racism. This seems apparent in a number of the cases discussed in our case studies of boxing, cricket, football and other sports. They all contain examples of 'fans' abusing or applying racial stereotypes to sports stars who they would never have any genuine expectation of physically encountering. Social media, such as Twitter, provides members of the public with the kind of remote, direct access that would allow racism to take place, while not affording the more intimate, physical engagement that might inhibit such racism.

In short, anonymity, feelings of invisibility/privacy, quick response time, a lack of personal information about the recipient and a lack of previous contact with the recipient all contribute towards feelings of disinhibition on social media. And, according to Suler (2004), these factors of disinhibition exacerbate anti-social behaviour online.

### *Personality*

Personality types are also significant. Suler (2004) notes that for some people, the internet provides a space where our deeper intrapsychic thoughts are presented, whereas in the physical world, they remain hidden. Someone with repressed anger may vent their frustrations online, thereby revealing their inner thoughts. A shy person may only express flirtatious comments in cyberspace as this invisibility aids disinhibition. And a teenager may post a racial epithet online thus venting his/her frustration towards a minority ethnic group. Put simply, social media arguably allows a space for users to post their inner, more 'borderline' or, in some cases, 'abhorrent' thoughts (Hylton 2013: 14). As Suler (2004: 324) argues:

> The fact that some people report being more like their 'true self' while online reinforces this conceptual temptation. Inspired by Freud's archeo-logical model of the mind, these ideas rest on the assumption that personality structure is constructed in layers, that a core, true self exists beneath various layers of defenses and the more superficial roles of everyday social interactions.

That said, Suler (2004: 325) continues by suggesting that while a person may act differently online, they are still 'two-dimensions of that same person, each revealed within a different situational context'. In other words, a different setting or context allows us to see a different part of one's identity.

Social media thus provides a platform for users to express their true feel-ings; feelings that might be considered too risqué in the physical world. It also allows users the opportunity to be a more confident version of their physical beings. Hence, social network sites harbour many positives as, for instance, they encourage confidence and promote free speech and equality. That said, Crandall and Eshleman (2003) postulate that those who harbour a lack of empathy, low self-esteem and are generally anti-social are more likely to post racist discourse online. In addition, Suler (2004) argues that 'dissociative imagination', i.e. one's belief that the internet is merely a game to be played, aids anti-social behaviour online.

For some users then, there appears to be a 'lexical ladder of acceptability'. At the bottom of this ladder is the physical world. Here, it is generally believed to be unacceptable to overtly express hate speech. In turn, we may suppress our desires to stereotype and racialise individuals and groups (Bodenhausen *et al.* 2009; Crandall and Eshleman 2003; Zarate 2009) because of our 'external motivation' (Plant and Devine 1998). As previously stated, articulating prejudice overtly is suppressed due to our 'situational vulnerability'. Within the public sphere, racist, fascist and sexist views are considered unacceptable.

Conversely, the digital public sphere has provided a new platform for some people to express hateful messages (ICCA 2013). Worryingly, some online users perceive social media to be a suitable place to express racism. Whereas the physical world may represent a space whereby rules, conventions and laws must be obeyed, cyberspace, according to some users, is a game in which different rules apply. Social media is placed at the top of the 'lexical ladder', as, for some, hateful discourse is deemed acceptable. Social network sites are thus considered separate to 'real life', as anti-social behaviour and trolling is perceived to be 'a bit of fun'. In sum, the personality of the offender must be scrutinised as well as other factors, as those who harbour a lack of empathy view social media within the parameters of 'dissociative imagination' and posses low self-esteem are more likely to racially abuse fellow social network users.

### *Condition*

It has been noted that if one is stressed, drunk or is enduring an episode of heightened emotion, they will be more prone to espousing racism online. As Crandall and Eshleman (2003: 425) posit, alcohol acts as a stimulant which aids disinhibition. The Liam Stacey case study, and many of the offenders discussed in Chapter 5, are cases in point.

In addition, if we are in a state of heightened emotion or are feeling threatened, it is likely that racism will be evoked as a reactionary mechanism (Bodenhausen *et al.* 2009). But, we must again stress that social media racism is deposited with a little more cognition due to the slight time-lag. As Bodenhausen *et al.* (2009: 112) note, 'when people have the luxury of abundant time and free attention, they can carefully consider how they wish to respond and make conscious, intentional choices to guide their social reactions'. With the benefit of time, we can make calculated decisions with regards to what we publish. But, in the world of sport, emotion and passion can supersede our ability to consider the acceptability of our discourse. Hateful tweets are thus sent in the 'heat of the moment' (Long and Hylton 2002; Rowe 2004). Because Twitter relies on the immediacy of posts, it is unlikely that users will actually consider the full extent of their social reactions.

For some sports fans then, condition acts as a stimulant of racism. Reactionary racism posted in the 'heat of the moment' (Long and Hylton 2002; Rowe 2004) is therefore a causal factor and, according to the ICCA (2013), it can lead to mob dynamics.

> In mob dynamics, groups with homogenous views become more extreme as the members' interactions reinforce preexisiting views; people start to lose their individuality, which encourages them to act on 'destructive impulses'; groups encourage their members to view their victims as lacking humanity and personal identity, leaving them to be more destructive toward their targets; and group members becomes more aggressive if they perceive that authority figures are supporting their efforts.
>
> (ICCA 2013: 12)

Condition can thus encourage a mob mentality. This can be observed with the NHL case study of Joel Ward and his treatment on Twitter following his series-winning goal against the Boston Bruins. Arguably, if social norms are weak, as well as penalties/punishments, mob dynamics are more likely to flourish. The condition of the user, whether it be stressed, tired, threatened, distracted or drunk, can all encourage racism on social media.

## Recommendations

This section shall present a number of recommendations that we believe would help challenge and reduce racism on social media. However, this is not an easy task as social media is a complex phenomenon that transcends nations and legal systems. Therefore, it must be pointed out that we approach this task from a UK perspective, while we also understand that some of our recommendations have certain limitations.

### *Social network sites*

As Chapter 3 suggested, social network sites such as Twitter and Facebook have guidelines on what they constitute as hate speech. Yet, for many social network sites, the process of reporting hate speech has traditionally been lengthy, confusing and somewhat tedious. Nonetheless, progress was observed in August 2013 as Twitter finally agreed to devote more time and energy into challenging racism by introducing a report abuse button. Facebook's policy is arguably easier to navigate as it provides a 'help center' which includes the following links: How to report things; report a violation, bullying, tools for addressing abuse; contact your grievance officer, etc. And YouTube, a site that relies on user-generated content, also provides a 'policy center' which defines what is considered acceptable and unacceptable speech. YouTube encourages free speech but it strongly refutes hate speech which promotes violence or hatred against individuals or groups based on certain attributes such as race or ethnic origin, religion, disability, etc. There is a tool for 'reporting hateful content' whereby users can be blocked and videos can be flagged.

Action, however belated it may be, is now being taken by leading social network sites regarding combating hate speech. Encouragingly, they offer examples of unacceptable conduct and signpost users to 'report' pages. Yet, this process could be even easier and streamlined. The ICCA (2013: 35) remain critical, as

> Intermediaries should make it easy to utilize the collective efforts of their users to identify and limit hate speech. Intermediaries should have easy-to-find and easy-to-use reporting mechanisms that allow users to report hate speech that violates the terms of service.

Moreover, despite some improvements, it is fundamental that users are instructed in how to efficiently report abuse in a manner that social network sites, or specifically the 'moderators', can understand and process quickly. This raises a number of significant questions, though. Who decides what is and what is not racist? What training do these moderators undertake? Do these moderators have the time and skills to accurately determine whether racism has been espoused? Are they realistically able to decipher whether a single flagged post is racist if it is observed out of context?

When we consider the constant stream of uploaded status', photos and videos on social media, the enormity of the moderators' task becomes evident. Around 500 million tweets are posted every day (Holt 2012). Statistics show that Facebook has over 1.11 billion monthly active users (Lee 2012). More than 1 billion unique users visit YouTube each month with over 100 hours of footage being uploaded every minute (**www.youtube.com/yt/press/en-GB/statistics.html**). Instagram, despite operating on a smaller scale, boasts 150 million active users who post an average of 55 million images a day (**http://instagram.com/press/**). As the ICCA (2013: 25) state:

> It is not always obvious to an intermediary or its employees what constitutes hate speech and how to adjudicate amongst competing claims. Furthermore, the problem of scale … and the volume of complaints received means that reviewers may have mere seconds to make a historical, contextual, political and social determination about the message before them.

Facebook's definition of hate speech arguably complicates the matter further as they aim to distinguish 'between serious and humorous speech' (**www. facebook.com/help/359033794168099/**). This is perhaps a cause for concern, as academics, politicians, public figures, comedians and so on routinely struggle to agree on what is banter and what is racism (Burdsey 2011b). And, due to the communicative differences between online and offline interaction, how can we prove whether comments were posted with a sarcastic, humorous or serious intention?

Put simply, social network sites and their moderators have an extremely difficult task; a task that requires time, context and a firm conceptual understanding of racism. However, moderators are not afforded this luxury as they may be confronted with hundreds of flagged posts per day. Moderators thus have to make snap decisions regarding highly contentious material – either it is racist, or it is not. One could suggest that social network sites should therefore devote more time, energy and recourses to this area. For the following interviewee: 'Social media companies have a special responsibility. They should be prohibiting, monitoring and policing expressions of racist sentiment' (Interview with criminologist and hate speech specialist 15 November 2013). As the ICCA (2013: 35) note then, social network sites should filter posts. However, because it is not possible to filter all content, resources and mechanisms should be enforced to 'monitor, respond to complaints about, and remove hate speech in a manner that preserves free expression and innovation while respecting the terms of service'.

It could be suggested that social network sites should implement an algorithm to screen or identify racist or racial terms. As Bartlett *et al.* (2014) found, 10,000 racial, religious and ethnic slurs are posted every day on Twitter. However, it is estimated that up to 70 per cent of these posts use such terms in non-derogatory ways. Nonetheless, these figures still emphasise that 'Twacism' is worthy of serious attention and debate as 2,000 racist tweets occur daily. An algorithm could therefore be used to identify potentially inappropriate or offensive language such as 'nigga', 'Coon' or 'Paki' (Bartlett *et al.* 2014) before the comment can be posted. Hence, users that include any racial term programmed under the algorithm should be presented with an additional 'Are You Sure?' box before they can execute the command. Although this may be frustrating for users who aim to express such terms in solidarity, this additional filter gives some potential offenders the opportunity to reconsider their actions before posting. This 'Are You Sure?' addition would be explained under the social networks' terms of service so that users understand why their potential post has been flagged. This addition to social media makes sense and is arguably inexpensive to create, develop and enforce. If this acted as a deterrent, it would also lighten the workload for social media moderators.

It could be argued that social network sites should remove the option of anonymity as this function encourages disinhibition and therefore anti-social behaviour (Crandall and Eshleman 2003; Hylton 2013; Suler 2004). If this function was removed, users would no longer be able to hide 'backstage' (Feagin 2010) as their 'real' identities would be open for all to see. It has been found that 'online public identification has stopped much cyberhate as anonymity is mask from behind which much hate is spewed' (ICCA 2013: 33). If anonymity was removed, social media would represent a transparent platform. This would mean that offenders could be tracked and dealt with in greater ease.

However, there are fundamental issues with this recommendation. First of all, although anonymity can encourage racism on social media, there have been many cases in which offenders have used their real names. For example @liamstacey9 and @joshuacryer from Chapter 5. Thus, removing anonymity would not simply solve the problem. Second, it could be argued that anonymity protects democracy and freedom. Anonymity online has made it possible for free speech to break through the physical barriers imposed by totalitarian regimes. Anonymity also allows people the opportunity to discuss somewhat embarrassing or sensitive topics such as sex and medical or mental health without facing any negative ramifications in their everyday lives. In short, anonymity represents a 'double-edged sword' as it 'has been very important to political dissidents, religious minorities and radical thinkers' (ICCA 2013: 33). Anonymity is an important function in the social media world and although revoking it would perhaps reduce incidents of racism, we believe that it would be unwise and should remain in place.

Social network sites should be more transparent and collaborate in creating and developing a more coherent and consistent policy with regards to what is acceptable and what is unacceptable behaviour. Social network sites should also publicly speak out and condemn incidents involving hate speech. As the ICCA (2013: 35) state:

> Intermediaries should provide users with information about how decisions are made with respect to the removal or non-removal of hate speech that violates the terms of service. While it is probable that individualized responses to complaints would be difficult, intermediaries can increase transparency by publishing case studies and/or genera examples of speech that has been deemed unacceptable under the terms of service.

Stan Collymore, a former professional footballer, publicly criticised Twitter in January 2014 for not acting after he received racist tweets and death threats. Twitter failed to comment on the incident due to their policy guidelines. For Collymore, although the police were 'fantastic', Twitter was guilty of ' "hiding behind" its rules about not commenting on individual cases' (**www.bbc.co.uk/news/uk-25838114**). Instead of publicly condemning the treatment of Collymore, Twitter simply released a generic policy statement. Nonetheless, we must understand that social network sites cannot respond to every single case. Thus, as the ICCA (2013) suggest, publishing annual reports which highlight case studies would be a positive step forward. This would allow users an insight into what social network sites consider acceptable and unacceptable behaviour. If a broad selection of cases are included, there would be less pressure on social network sites to respond to individual cases such as the Stan Collymore case.

In sum, social network sites should join together to create a more holistic policy regarding hate speech. An annual report should be published which includes a broad range of case studies, examples and information concerning how to report incidents quickly and effectively. The process of reporting abuse, across all sites, needs to be reconsidered and made more streamlined. Moderators, as we have suggested, have an extremely difficult task. It could be suggested that these employees must have specialist knowledge of the law (country dependant), hate speech and must also be aware of the complexities of 'race' and racism. Moreover, these employees should be given further time to respond to incidents and follow up any additional lines of enquiries. They should also have a direct pathway, link or contact with the police if an incident is deemed illegal. An algorithm, however, could make a positive contribution and in turn, lighten the workload for moderators. Finally, anonymity constitutes a grey area as removing this would arguably help reduce hate speech on social media. But, there are many positives to this function, as it promotes free speech and democracy. Thus, educating users on social media and challenging social norms would be a better step forward than revoking the option of anonymity.

### *Education*

According to Crandall and Eshleman (2003: 419), 'the sheer variety of fountainheads of prejudice reveals the difficulty of eliminating prejudice altogether'. In other words, racism is one of many diseases which has struggled to find a cure. This is because prejudice and stereotyping are complex, multideterminated processes that are influenced by nature and nurture. Our brains have evolved to efficiently process large amounts of information that comes to us every day. In order to make sense of this data, we tend to categorise or cluster information. These categories assist us in making quick judgements so that we do not have to think about how to react to every unique person or situation. This is helpful in times of threat. But, these snap judgements, or stereotypes, can often be inaccurate and sometimes harmful.

Nurture aids prejudicial thinking as 'children learn prejudices from their parents' (Crandall and Eshleman 2003: 418). Moreover, we also learn our prejudicial beliefs from the mass media (Crandall and Eshleman 2003; Hartmann and Husband 1974; Malik 2002). 'Film, television, and the Web not only create the relevant stereotypes, but more importantly, they provide us with the relevant social norms – who we can and cannot be' (Stangor 2009: 9). We can, however, become non-prejudiced, as education and social cohesion can assist in this battle. These two factors are championed by anti-racist organisation, Show Racism the Red Card:

> The way in which we tackle racism in general is by educating young people … If you try to elicit positive change in someone it's always possibly best to get someone who is of a mindset while they are still learning … across the UK we work with around about 35,000 young people every year, plus we educate thousands of teachers about racism every year.
>
> (Interview with Craig Bankhead, North East Education Manager, Show Racism the Red Card, 14 March 2011)

Raising young people's awareness, knowledge and understanding of different socio-cultural groups outside their own is particularly a positive step forward. This view is expressed by Bodenhausen *et al.* (2009: 129) who note that 'the creation of diverse environments is the best avenue for long-term prejudice reduction. To increase the diversity of many environments … it is necessary to increase the participation of members of underrepresented and typically devalued groups'. If physical societies become more socially cohesive, it is likely that this will be mirrored by digital communities (Boyd 2011: 220).

Furthermore, better educating children and parents about social media use could be a positive step forward if we are to challenge racism on social network sites. The UK Council for Child Internet Safety (UKCCIS) is a voluntary organisation that brings together over 200 organisations from across government, industry, law, academia and charity sectors that strive to keep children safe online. The UKCCIS's aim is to raise awareness and protect children from cyber-bullying, harmful content, sexual images, loss of privacy and scams. The organisation has created a code of practice which was formulated by service providers following a consultation about parental internet controls. Significantly, the UKCCIS also provide industry advice on social networking and moderation. Nevertheless, although this endorsement highlights that the government are aware of the dangers that children face online, 'the Government has yet to institute an explicit policy that requires educating children about internet hate' (ICCA 2013: 27).

In short, the educational system cannot be underestimated as:

> ...education systems can play a pivotal role in countering Internet hate speech by educating young people on how to identify Internet hate speech. Educating youth to identify Internet hate, the perils of it and the impact it has, can act as a deterrent against promulgating it further.
>
> (ICCA 2013: 28)

Educating young people in an educational environment where they are still learning appears to be the correct setting to engage in and discuss issues concerning hate speech in the physical and online world. Importantly, children and teachers will be able to understand what constitutes hate speech and will be able to successfully report it. As the ICCA (2013: 29) add: 'Once children can identify hate speech, they can be empowered to combat it'. It is also hoped that education and social cohesion groups can help to further encourage a dialogue between majority and minority communities. Communication between diverse groups can increase empathy levels, while it also gives potential offenders the opportunity to gain insight and understanding of other communities.

### The law

The task of policing and prosecuting any internet-related crime is fraught with difficulties. These include the vast scale of the content, often limited resources, inconsistencies across legal systems and the problems of tackling often internationally wide offences through national-based law enforcement authorities. As Yar (2013: 16) states: 'Crimes in cyberspace bring together offenders, victims and targets that may well be physically situated in different countries and continents, and so the offence spans national territories and boundaries.'

Furthermore, there is no unitary, single or shared law concerning internet hate speech, as every country across the world has its own law regarding acceptable and unacceptable discourse. Each country has their own definition of what constitutes hate speech, and while some countries, such as India, ascertain a capacious definition, America offers 'strong jurisprudential protection of speech' (ICCA 2013: 20). Dr Jeni Kubota, of New York University, highlights the American perspective on social media and law:

> In the United States it has been difficult to prosecute individuals for hate speech in public. This makes it difficult to enforce or prevent racism on social media. The legal battles over hate speech on the Internet and in the news have not fared well in court.
>
> (Interview 4 October 2013)

The UK similarly encourages freedom of expression. However, social media users guilty of using unacceptable language may face repercussions under section 127 of the Communications Act 2003. Since the rise of social media, charges under this act have significantly increased. Additionally, internet users can also face punishment under the Malicious Communications Act 1988.

As Chapter 3 highlighted, the Crown Prosecution Service (CPS) have issued new guidelines regarding prosecuting social media users. Credible threats of violence, harassment and breaches of court order will be tackled 'robustly'. Yet, somewhat alarmingly, the CPS have omitted hate speech (racism, fascism, sexism, homophobia, etc.) from their three primary focuses. Having said that, they add that 'grossly offensive' material, i.e. hate speech, will be challenged. But, because the CPS view social media communication as different from the physical world, offenders who display remorse or regret are likely to escape prosecution.

From the police's perspective, we must understand the enormity of the task as they deal with social media abuse cases on a regular basis (Bartlett *et al.* 2014; BBC Online 19 September 2013). Cases look set to increase, especially when we consider recent research findings which show that one in five young people suffer extreme bullying on social network sites (BBC Online 11 August 2013). But, because social media users have the platform to reach a far wider audience, does this mean that offenders should face a higher criminal penalty? An expert in criminology and hate speech suggests that:

> The use of law is important as it sends a powerful message. I don't necessarily think that it deters potential offenders but it does send a message to targeted communities that the rest of the nation, the rest of society, society generally, refutes these sentiments enough that laws are being enacted ... [But] they shouldn't necessarily get a higher penalty in terms of criminal sanction but I think they need something else. There are some imaginative schemes that work with racist offenders that get them to try and understand the impact of what they're doing; the impact of their sentiments when they express them, on the basis that they might think twice about doing it again ... There's more hope in the humanistic approach by trying to get offenders and potential offenders, in preventative schemes, to try to help them appreciate what it's like to be on the receiving end to kind of generate some empathy for victims or potential victims, on the basis that if you can understand it, it can prevent them from those impulses; prevent them from offending.
>
> (Interview 22 October 2013)

Research certainly suggests that the social norms will affect the likelihood of racism and other forms of prejudice being expressed within that context.

The laws, and enforcement of those laws, that apply within that context are one of the means through which social norms are developed (Plant and Devine 1998). In other words, if potential social media offenders feel there is a genuine chance of them being caught and prosecuted for their online behaviour, this is likely to have an impact on that behaviour. It remains to be seen what new UK prosecuting guidelines will mean for the number of cases being brought to court each year. While 'race' remains an aggravating factor, there appears to be a move away from prosecuting individual or sporadic cases of abuse, towards focusing on more prolonged cases of harassment or genuine, immediate threats of violence. Whatever happens, for prosecutions to be effective as a deterrent, potential offenders must believe there is a realistic chance of being caught. This requires increased determination and resources on behalf of relevant authorities.

For example, there is some initial evidence to suggest that Kick It Out's new reporting app has helped to bring about a significant increase in the number of complaints about racist behaviour. Such a move is to be welcomed and could be imitated by other sports and anti-racism organisations. Similarly, key sports authorities, such as the FA and PFA in the case of football, need to do more to advise athletes on issues of social media racism, and to encourage and support them in reporting online abuse.

However, such action can only be effective if complemented by corresponding changes in the approach of the police and prosecuting authorities. The police are already struggling to cope with the volume of social media-related incidents. Any increase in the number of cases being reported to the police will need to be backed up with more police resources being devoted to this issue. If, as the Home Office figures show, arrests for racially aggravated offences have been reduced within sports stadiums, perhaps resources now need to be redeployed to where racism has found a new outlet – social media. Racism has, to some extent, been managed in sporting arenas thanks to the application of law and greater presence of the police – similar tactics now need to be applied to manage it better online.

### *Confrontation*

Zarate (2009: 398) argues that 'for many reasons, openly challenging racist comments might very well prove to have long-term benefits'. As previously noted, Stan Collymore encounters 'Twacism' regularly. But Collymore usually makes the habit of screen-shotting, re-tweeting and reporting racially offensive comments. For example, on 6 January 2014, Collymore re-tweeted a screen-shot of three twitter users that had made anti-Semitic comments following Spurs' 2–0 defeat by Arsenal. Within 48 hours, his post, which led with: 'Hope Twitter/police take action', was re-tweeted almost 2,000 times and 'favourited' by over 600 users.

This indicates that role models, such as Collymore, and his followers, are likely to confront racism by re-tweeting. Moreover, this united front against racism promotes the idea of inclusivity in cyberspace. Exposing social media users who have broken the terms of service demonstrates that racism is unacceptable and will not be tolerated. Therefore, social media users have an important role to play in the fight against racism. The advice is often given – 'do not feed the trolls' – as reaction and publicity is often what they seek. However, the social norms of particular online contexts can be created by their users. While the internet offers bigots the opportunity to find like-minded bigots, it also creates the potential for their views to be contested. There is evidence to suggest that such contest has the potential to affect, or at the very least inhibit, the potential of racist behaviour. In other words, the advice should be: do not ignore the trolls – but challenge and report them, as every single user has the ability to confront racism. If racism is tackled collectively, hate speech should decrease and trolls will reconsider posting material that is deemed exclusionary.

On the other hand, D'Andrea and Daniels (1999: 97) suggest that some white people refrain from challenging racism because they feel they may 'not be taken seriously or would be met with defensive reactions by many White people they knew'. Speaking out against racism thus requires a certain confidence, as doing so may isolate or alienate the complainant within his/her in-group. Those who report online racism also run the risk of being labelled part of the 'PC gone mad' brigade. For some offenders and likewise thinkers, acceptable language is challenged. As a result, the abuse sometimes diverts to the complainant. These factors arguably prohibit less confident users from challenging and reporting social media racism.

Nonetheless, if we unite in combating racism on social media we can make this a positive space. It is thus hoped that offences will decline over time but we must also be aware that some offenders simply enjoy the oxygen of publicity.

## Conclusion

This book, through its various case studies and observations, has demonstrated that sports-related racism on social media is a problem that deserves and demands attention. We have critically examined a number of factors that are likely to increase or encourage hate speech on social media. There is no single explanation but a complex network of factors. For example, the nature of communication represents a clear difference between the physical and digital worlds, as disinhibition features such as anonymity, invisibility and privacy can be afforded in online spaces. Condition, personality type and social context are also important factors when considering causes of racism on social media.

There is no unitary policy that can be put forward when challenging racism on social network sites due to the complex nature of the issue. Our response, as this chapter has demonstrated, is multi-faceted. First of all, education is paramount and the only way to genuinely address the issue of racism in our society. An understanding of racism, its various historical and modern day forms, and the everyday impacts it has on people's lives should form an integral part of the education curriculum. Similarly, we need better education about using and being safe in online worlds. Organisations such as the UKCCIS should continue to educate and inform children, parents and teachers about how to safely use the internet and social media, while also highlighting how to identify and effectively report racism, and other forms of hate speech, on social network sites. Such sites must also take a greater degree of responsibility in the fight to reduce hate speech. Ideally, it would be beneficial if social network sites joined together to publish a shared terms of service as well as an annual report about racist and other forms of abuse. These organisations should be more proactive and responsible in addressing issues and more helpful to law enforcement when necessary. The reporting process must be more streamlined and should be as easy to use as the plat-forms' other functions. Meanwhile, sports and anti-racism organisations need to do their bit by encouraging and supporting people in highlighting and reporting offences online – the initial success of Kick It Out's reporting app is an example of what could be done. Athletes also need better advice and guidance on this specific issue from their relevant professional and sporting authorities. Such moves then need to be backed up with more effective policing of this matter. There needs to be a more consistent and coherent approach to social media crimes across police forces, and more resources need to be assigned. To some extent, racism has moved from the physical to the online world and the allocation of resources needs to reflect this.

If there has been an air of complacency about racism in sport, there has been an air of bewilderment about sport, racism and social media. At times, sporting and legal authorities have seemed confused by the speed, volume and nature of the issues social media has thrown their way. There have been some real positives to this, such as the loosening of PR's control over the flow of information, or the greater engagement between sports people and their audiences. However, one of the negatives has undoubtedly been a flood of racist content and abuse.

In our end is our beginning. Racism will exist in sport and on social media as long as it exists in society. It is best addressed through education and, unfortunately slow, social change. This is the only way to genuinely address the underlying causes of the problem. The symptoms, though, can also be treated. Football, along with other sports, may have become complacent about racism, but it has managed the problem and changed, at least for some, the experience of being involved in the sport. Racism has found a new outlet in social media and now this needs to be tackled in a genuine and determined way.

# References

Abbas, T. (2007) 'British Muslim minorities today: challenges and opportunities to Europeanism, multiculturalism and Islamism', *Sociology Compass*, 1, 2: 720–736.

Alexander, C. and Knowles, C. (2005) 'Introduction', in C. Alexander and C. Knowles (eds) *Making Race Matter: Bodies, Space and Identity*, Basingstoke: Palgrave Macmillan.

Allen, C. (2007) 'Islamophobia and its consequences', in S. Amghar, A. Boubekeur and M. Emerson (eds) *European Islam: Challenges for Public Policy and Society*, Brussels: Centre for European Policy Studies.

Allen, K. (2012) 'Caps' ward: racist tweets "didn't ruin my day"', *USA Today*, 26 April, http://usatoday30.usatoday.com/sports/hockey/nhl/story/2012-04-26/joel-ward-interview/54557232/1.

Allport, G.W. (1954) The Nature of Prejudice, Cambridge, MA: Perseus Books.

Anderson, K.J. (2010) *Benign Bigotry: The Psychology of Subtle Prejudice*, Cambridge: Cambridge University Press.

Ansari, H. (2003) *Muslims in Britain*, London: Minority Rights Group.

Archer, L. (2006) 'Muslim adolescents in Europe', *European Issues in Children's Identity and Citizenship*, 22, 2: 55–69.

Back, L., Crabbe, T. and Solomos, J. (2001) *The Changing Face of Football: Racism, Identity and Multiculture in the English Game*, Oxford: Berg.

Barker, M. (1981) *The New Racism: Conservatives and the Ideology of the Tribe*, London: Alethia books.

Barnes, S. (1990) 'The importance of being too earnest', *The Times*, 12 April.

Bartlett, J., Reffin, J., Rumball, N. and Williamson, S. (2014) *Anti-Social Media*, London: Demos.

Bauman, Z. (1988) 'Exit visas and entry tickets: the paradoxes of Jewish assimilation', *Telos*, 77: 45–77.

BBC Online (2012, 22 February) 'David Cameron pledges to "crush" racism in football', www.bbc.co.uk/sport/0/football/17124938.

BBC Online (2012, 22 May) 'Liam Stacey "sorry" for racist Muamba tweets', www.bbc.co.uk/news/uk-wales-18165854.

BBC Online (2012, 30 July) 'Olympics football: Michel Morganella expelled for racist tweet', www.bbc.co.uk/sport/0/olympics/19054995.

BBC Online (2012, 17 August) 'Rio Ferdinand fined for Ashley Cole "choc ice" tweet', www.bbc.co.uk/sport/0/football/18847477.

BBC Online (2013, 29 July) 'Twitter must do more to stop abuse, says police chief', www.bbc.co.uk/news/uk-23493106.

BBC Online (2013, 3 August) 'Twitter's Tony Wang issues apology to abuse victims', www.bbc.co.uk/news/uk-23559605.

BBC Online (2013, 11 August) 'One in five children bullied online, says NSPCC survey', www.bbc.co.uk/news/uk-23654329.

BBC Online (2013, 19 September) 'Twitter trolling on the rise, the Met says', www.bbc.co.uk/news/uk-england-london-24160004.

BBC Online (2014, 22 January) 'Ex-footballer Collymore accuses Twitter over abusive messages', www.bbc.co.uk/news/uk-25838114.

Bell, C. (1980) 'Racism: a symptom of the narcissistic personality disorder', *Journal of National Medical Association*, 72, 7: 661–665.

Bell, D.A. (1980) 'Brown v. board of education and the interest-convergence dilemma', *Harvard Law Review*, 93: 518–533.

Bernasconi, R. (2009) 'Who invented the concept of race?', in L. Back and J. Solomos (eds) *Theories of Race and Racism: A Reader*, second edition, Oxon: Routledge.

Bernstein, A. and Blain, N. (2003) 'Sport and the media: the emergence of a major research field', in A. Bernstein and N. Blain (eds) *Sport, Media, Culture: Global and Local Dimensions*, London: Frank Cass.

Bienkov, A. (2013) 'Police struggling as trolling offences soar', Politics.co.uk, 19 September, at M. Billig (1995) *Banal Nationalism*, London: Sage.

Billig, M. (1978) *Fascists: A Social Psychological View of the National Front*, London: Academic Press.

Bodenhausen, G.V., Todd, A.R. and Richardson, J.A. (2009) 'Controlling prejudice and stereotyping: antecedents, mechanisms and contexts', in Todd D. Nelson (ed.) *Handbook of Prejudice, Stereotyping and Discrimination*, New York: Taylor and Francis.

Bourdieu, P. (1977) *Outline of a Theory of Practice*, Cambridge: Cambridge University Press.

Bourdieu, P. (1984) *Distinction: A Social Critique of the Judgement of Taste*, London: Routledge.

Bowcott, O. (2012) 'Student who abused Fabrice Muamba on Twitter "should not have been jailed"', *Guardian*, 1 April, www.guardian.co.uk/uk/2012/apr/01/twitter-jailing-wrong-thomas-hammarberg.

Boyd, D. (2009) 'Social media is here to stay ... now what?', *Microsoft Research Tech Fest*, 26 February, Washington: Redmond.

Boyd, D. (2011) 'White flight in networked publics? How race and class shaped American teen engagement with MySpace and Facebook', in Lisa Nakamura and Peter Chow-White (eds) *Race After the Internet*, London: Routledge, 203–222.

Boyle, R. and Haynes, R. (2000) *Power Play: Sport, the Media and Popular Culture*, Essex: Pearson Education Ltd.

Brookes, R. (2002) *Representing Sport*, London: Arnold.

Buckels, E., Trapnell, P.D. and Paulhus, D.L. (2014) 'Trolls just want to have fun', *Personality and Individual Differences*, 67: 97–102.

Burdsey, D. (2007) *British Asians and Football: Culture, Identity, Exclusion*, Oxon: Routledge.

Burdsey, D. (2010) 'British Muslim experiences in English first-class cricket', *International Review for the Sociology of Sport*, 45, 3: 315–334.

Burdsey, D. (2011a) 'They think it's all over ... it isn't yet: the persistence of structural racism and racialised exclusion in twenty-first century football', in D. Burdsey (ed.) *Race, Ethnicity and Football: Persisting Debates and Emergent Issues*, New York: Routledge.

Burdsey, D. (2011b) 'That joke isn't funny anymore: racial microaggressions, color-blind ideology and the mitigation of racism in English men's first-class cricket', *Sociology of Sport Journal*, 28: 261–283.

Byrne, P. (2013) 'Bolton Wanderers striker has phone taken off him to help beat Twitter "obsession"', *Mirror Online*, 7 January, www.mirror.co.uk/sport/football/news/bolton-wanderers-striker-marvin-sordell-1523603.

Carmichael, S. and Hamilton, C. (1967) *Black Power: The Politics of Liberation in America*, New York: Vintage Books.

Carrington, B. (2010) *Race, Sport and Politics: The Sporting Black Diaspora*, London: Sage Publications.

Cashmore, E. (2005) *Making Sense of Sports*, fourth edition, Oxon: Routledge.

Cashmore, E. and Troyna, B. (1983) *Introduction to Race Relations*, second edition, London: Routledge & Kegan Paul.

Cazenave, N.A. and Maddern, D.A. (1999) 'Defending the white race: white male faculty opposition to a "white racism" course', *Race and Society*, 2: 25–50.

Chalmers, A.F. (1982) *What is This Thing Called Science? An Assessment of the Nature and Status of Science and its Methods*, second edition, Milton Keynes: Open University Press.

Chun, W.H.K. (2012) 'Race and/as technology, or how to do things race', in Lisa Nakamura and Peter A. Chow-White (eds) *Race After the Internet*, New York: Routledge.

Coates, R.D. (2011a) 'Covert racism: an introduction', in Rodney D. Coates (ed.) *Covert Racism: Theories, Institutions and Experiences*, Leiden: Hotei Publishing.

Coates, R.D. (2011b) 'Covert racism in an age of color blindness!', www.thisweekinsociology.com/2011/10/covert-racism-in-age-of-color-blindness.html.

Cohen, P. (1996) 'Homing devices', in V. Amit-Talai and C. Knowles (eds) *Re-Situating Identities: The Politics of Race, Ethnicity and Culture*, Hadleigh: Broadview.

Collymore, S. (2014) 'Stan Collymore: "Twitter a vacuum for abuse"', BBC News, 22 January, www.bbc.co.uk/news/uk-25839299.

Cottle, S. (2004) *The Racist Murder of Stephen Lawrence: Media Performance and Public Transformation*, London: Praeger.

Cottle, S. (2006) *Mediatized Conflict*, Buckingham, UK: Open University Press.

Coyle, D. (2010) *The Talent Code: Greatness isn't Born, it's Grown*, London: Arrow Books.

Crandall, C.S. and Eshleman, A. (2003) 'A justification-suppression model of the expression and experience of prejudice', *Psychological Bulletin*, 129, 3: 414–446.

Culture, Media and Sport Committee (2012) 'Racism in football: second report of session 2012–2013', www.sportdevelopment.info/index.php/subjects/57-football/827-racism-in-football-second-report-of-session-201213.

D'Andrea, M. and Daniels, J. (1999) 'Exploring the psychology of white racism through naturalistic inquiry', *Journal of Counselling & Development*, 77: 93–101.

Daily Record (2014) 'Twitter troll jailed for race hate tweets against Rangers stars', 9 January, www.dailyrecord.co.uk/news/scottish-news/twitter-troll-jailed-race-hate-3003472.

*Daily Telegraph* (Australia) (2013) 'Hope rises from Ashes', 25 June.

Darwin, C.R. (1859) *On the Origin of Species by Means of Natural Selection, or the Preservation of Favoured Races in the Struggle for Life*, first edition, London: John Murray.

Davies, G.A. (2011) 'Amir Khan furious at overzealous US immigration', *Telegraph*, 9 June, www.telegraph.co.uk/sport/othersports/boxing/amir-khan/8566662/Amir-Khan-furious-at-overzealous-US-immigration.html.

De John, I. and Kennedy, H. (2012) 'Jeremy Lin headline slur was "honest mistake", fired ESPN editor Anthony Federico claims', *Daily News*, 20 February, www.nydailynews.com/entertainment/tv-movies/jeremy-lin-slur-honest-mistake-fired-espn-editor-anthony-federico-claims-article-1.1025566.

Dirs, B. (2013) 'Amir Khan: why he just can't win over the doubters', BBC Online, 28 April, www.bbc.co.uk/sport/0/boxing/22327752.

Dirs, D. (2011) 'Mark Bright says racism is still a problem for football', BBC Online, 17 November, www.bbc.co.uk/sport/0/football/15744902.

Ditch the Label (2013) 'The annual cyberbullying survey 2013', www.ditchthelabel.org/annual-cyber-bullying-survey-cyber-bullying-statistics/.

Dovidio, J.F., Evans, N. and Tyler, R.B. (1986) 'Racial stereotypes: the content of their cognitive representations', *Journal Of Experimental Social Psychology*, 22: 22–37.

Dyer, R. (1997) *White*, London: Routledge.

Edwards, J. (2013) 'Facebook is no longer the most popular social network for teens', *Business Insider*, www.businessinsider.com/facebook-and-teen-user-trends-2013-10#!KvajP.

Elder, C. (2008) *Being Australian: Narratives of National Identity*, Sydney: Allen & Unwin.

ESPN Online (2011) 'Banana thrown at Wayne Simmonds', 23 September, http://espn.go.com/nhl/story/_/id/7007219/fan-throws-banana-philadelphia-flyers-winger-wayne-simmonds.

Evans, B. (2013) 'One in five young people suffer "extreme cyber-bullying" every day with Facebook accounting for more than half of the abuse', *Mail Online*, 2 October, www.dailymail.co.uk/news/article-2441239/1-5-young-people-suffer-extreme-cyber-bullying-day-Facebook-accounting-half.html.

Everett, A. (ed.) (2008) *Learning Race and Ethnicity: Youth and Digital Media*, Cambridge: The MIT Press.

Everett, A. (2009) *Digital Diaspora: A Race for Cyberspace*, New York: SUNY Press.

Everett, A. (2012) 'Have we become postracial yet? Race and media technology in the age of president Obama', in L. Nakamura and P. Chow-White (eds) *Race After the Internet*, London: Routledge, 146–167.

Express Online (2012) 'Hunt down these vile trolls', 31 March, www.express.co.uk/comment/columnists/richard-and-judy/311582/Hunt-down-these-vile-trolls.

Farquharson, K. and Marjoribanks, T. (2006) 'Representing Australia: race, the media and cricket', *Journal of Sociology*, 42, 1: 25–41.

Farrington, N., Kilvington, D., Price, J. and Saeed, A. (2012) *Race, Racism and Sports Journalism*, London: Routledge.

Feagin, J. (2010) *The White Racial Frame: Centuries of Racial Framing and Counter-Framing*, London: Routledge.

Fekete, L. (2002) *Racism, the Hidden Cost of September 11*, London: Institute of Race Relations.

FIFA.com (2011) 'FIFA against racism: a decade of milestones', 2 March, www.fifa.com/aboutfifa/socialresponsibility/news/newsid=1384919/

Fish, S. (1993) 'Reverse racism, or how the pot got to call the kettle black', www.theatlantic.com/magazine/archive/1993/11/reverse-racism-or-how-the-pot-got-to-call-the-kettle-black/304638/.

Fisher, D. (1990) 'Split between Britain, U.S. seen as "inevitable": foreign policy – the conservative party chairman fears that a "less European" America will provide the wedge', *Los Angeles Times*, 19 April.

Fiske, S.T. (2010) 'Are we born racist?', in Jason Marsh, Rodolfo Mendoza-Denton and Jeremy Adam Smith (eds) *Are We Born Racist? New Insights from Neuroscience and Positive Psychology*, Boston: Beacon Press.

Fiske, S.T. and Taylor, S.E. (1991) Social Cognition, New York: McGraw-Hill.

Fletcher, T. (2011) 'The making of English cricket cultures: empire, globalisation and (post) colonialism', *Sport in Society*, 14, 1: 17–36.

Freeman, H. (2012) 'Jeremy Lin row reveals deep-seated racism against Asian Americans', *Guardian*, 21 February.

Fuchs, C. (2014) *Social Media: A Critical Introduction*, London: Sage.

Gaertner, S. and Dovidio, J. (eds) (1986) 'The aversive form of racism', *Prejudice, Discrimination and Racism*, Orlando: Academic Press, 61–89.

Galloway, A.R. (2012) 'Does the Whatever Speak?', in L. Nakamura and P. Chow-White (eds) Race After the Internet, London: Routledge. pp. 111–127.

Gemmell, J. (2007) 'Cricket, race and the 2007 World Cup', *Sport in Society*, 10, 1: 1–10.

Gilroy, P. (1987) *'There ain't no Black in the Union Jack': The Cultural Politics of Race and Nation*, London: Routledge.

Gilroy, P. (1992) *Small Acts: Thoughts on the Politics of Black Cultures*, London: Serpent's Tail.

Glaser, J. and Kahn, K.B. (2005) 'Prejudice and discrimination and the internet', *The Social Psychology of the Internet*, 247–274.

Glaser, J., Dixit, J. and Green, D. (2002) 'Studying hate crime with the internet: what makes racists advocate racial violence?', *Journal of Social Issues*, 58, 1: 177–193.

Goldberg, S. (1990) 'Athletes: why blacks are better than whites', *International Journal of Sociology and Social Policy*, 10, 8: 67–79.

*Guardian* (2012) 'Teenagers given final warnings over racist tweets aimed at Sammy Ameobi', 7 February, www.guardian.co.uk/football/2012/feb/07/teenagers-warning-racist-tweets-sammy-ameobi.

Hall, S. (1990) 'Cultural identity and Diaspora', in J. Rutherford (ed.) *Identity: Culture, Community, Difference*, London: Lawrence and Wishart.

Hall, S. (1996) 'New ethnicities', in D. Morley and K.-H. Chen (eds) *Stuart Hall: Critical Dialogues in Cultural Studies*, London: Routledge, 441–449.

Hall, S. (1997) 'Introduction', in S. Hall (ed.) *Representation: Cultural Representations and Signifying Practices*, London: Sage.

Hampton, B. and Wellman, K. (1999) 'Living networked in a wired world', *Contemporary Sociology*, 28, 6 November: 648–654.

Hargiatti, E. (2012) 'Open doors, closed spaces? Differentiated adoption of social network sites by user background', in L. Nakamura and P. Chow-White (eds) *Race After the Internet*, London: Routledge, 223–245.

Hartmann, P. and Husband, C. (1974) *Racism and the Mass Media*, London: Davis-Poynter.

Hatfield, D. (1996) 'The Jack Nicklaus syndrome', *Humanist*, July–August, 1.

Hayes, M. (2013) 'Boof's the man', *Herald Sun*, 24 June.

Hebblethwaite, C. (2014) '#BBCtrending: why twitter is so big in Saudi Arabia', BBC News, www.bbc.co.uk/news/blogs-trending-25864558.

Herbert, I. (2014) 'Kick It Out reveals big increase in reports of abuse with social media providing a new outlet for racism and homophobia', 17 February, www.independent.co.uk/sport/football/premier-league/kick-it-out-reveals-big-increase-in-reports-of-abuse-with-social-media-providing-a-new-outlet-for-racism-and-homophobia-9124451.html.

Hill, K. (2012) 'Beware, tech abandoners: people without Facebook accounts are "suspicious"', www.forbes.com/sites/kashmirhill/2012/08/06/beware-tech-abandoners-people-without-facebook-accounts-are-suspicious/.

Hinton, S. and Hjorth, L. (2013) *Understanding Social Media*, London: Sage.

Hoberman, J. (1997) *Darwin's Athletes: How Sport has Damaged Black America and Presented the Myth of Race*, Boston: Houghton Mifflin Company.

Hodgson, A. (2014) 'England call up for Moeen Ali sparks racist slurs and nationality debate on Facebook', *The Standard*, 6 February.

Holden, G. (2008) 'World cricket as a postcolonial international society: IR meets the history of sport', *Global Society*, 22, 3: 337–368.

Holt, R. (2012) 'Twitter in numbers', *Telegraph*, 21 March, www.telegraph.co.uk/technology/twitter/9945505/Twitter-in-numbers.html.

Hook, D. (2006) '"Pre-discursive" racism', *Journal of Community & Applied Social Psychology*, 16: 207–232.

Howard, P.N. and Hussain, M.M. (2013) *Democracy's Fourth Wave? Digital Media and the Arab Spring*, Oxford: Oxford University Press.

Hylton, K. (2005) '"Race", sport and leisure: lessons from critical race theory', *Leisure Studies*, 24, 1: 81–98.

Hylton, K. (2009) *'Race' and Sport: Critical Race Theory*, London: Routledge.

Hylton, K. (2013) 'Dispositions to "race" and racism on the internet: online reactions to a 'racist' comment against Tiger Woods', CERS Working Paper, University of Leeds.

Instagram: http://instagram.com/press/.

Inter-Parliamentary Coalition for Combating Anti-Semitism (ICCA) (2013) 'Report by the task force on internet hate', 29 May.

James, C.L.R. (1963) *Beyond a Boundary*, London: Yellow Jersey Press.

James, W. (1993) 'Migration, racism and identity formations: the Caribbean experience in Britain', in W. James and C. Harris (eds) *Inside Babylon: The Caribbean Diaspora in Britain*, London: Verso.

Johnson, N. (2007) 'Building an integrated society', in M. Weatherell, M. Lafleche and R. Berkeley (eds) *Identity, Ethnic Diversity and Community Cohesion*, London: Sage.

Johnson, V.M.S. (2008) '"What then is the African American?" African and Afro-Caribbean identities in Black America', *Journal of American Ethnic History*, 28, 1: 77–103.

Kang, C. (2014) 'Twitter shares fall on weaker user growth', *Washington Post*, www.washingtonpost.com/business/technology/twitter-shares-fall-on-weak-user-growth/2014/02/05/aa11e932-8eaa-11e3-b227-12a45d109e03_story.html.

Kang, J. (2000) 'Cyber-race', *Harvard Law Review*, 113: 1130–1208.

Kawash, S. (1997) *Dislocating the Color Line*, Stanford: Stanford University Press.

Kick It Out (2013, 10 July) 'Non league footballer jailed for anti-Muslim Twitter posts', www.kickitout.org/news.php/news_id/5944.

Kick It Out (2013, 12 July) 'Mark McCammon cites "great advice" from Kick It Out as Facebook abuser bailed', www.kickitout.org/news.php/news_id/5945.

Kilvington, D. (2012) 'The "Asian frame", football and the sport media', *Networking Knowledge*, 5, 1: 201–218.

Kilvington, D. and Price, J. (2013) 'British Asians, overt racism and Islamophobia in English football', *International Journal of Sport and Society*, 3, 2: 169–180.

Kilvington, D., Farrington, N., Price, J. and Saeed, A. (2013) 'Black and white and read all over: institutional racism and sports media', *The International Journal of Sport and Society*, 3: 81–90.

Knox, M. (2003) 'Lehmann reveals the unwitting racism that infuses Australia', *The Age*, 26 January, http://theage.com.au/articles/2003/01/26/1043533952023.html.

Kohut, H. (1966) 'Forms and transformations of narcissism', *Journal of American Psychoanalytical Association*, 14: 243–272.

Kolko, B., Nakamura, L. and Rodman, G. (2000) *Race in Cyberspace*, London: Routledge.

Krotoski, A. (2013) *Untangling the Web: What the Internet is Doing to You*, London: Faber & Faber.

Lee, D. (2012) 'Facebook surpasses one billion users as it tempts new markets', BBC Online, 5 October, www.bbc.co.uk/news/technology-19816709#panel7.

Lewin, K. (1948) *Resolving Social Conflicts: Selected Papers on Group Dynamics*, New York: Harper & Row.

Lindsey, R.A. (2013) 'What the Arab spring tells us about the future of social media in revolutionary movements', *Small Wars Journal*, http://smallwarsjournal.com/jrnl/art/what-the-arab-spring-tells-us-about-the-future-of-social-media-in-revolutionary-movements.

Long, J. and Hylton, K. (2002) 'Shades of white: an examination of whiteness in sport', *Leisure Studies*, 21: 87–103.

Long, J., Carrington, B. and Spracklen, K. (1997) '"Asians cannot wear turbans in the scrum": explorations of racist discourse within professional rugby league', *Leisure Studies*, 16: 249–259.

Lovink, G. (2008) *Zero Comments: Blogging and Critical Internet Culture*, New York: Routledge.

Macmillan, D. (2012) 'Facebook rises as 63.5m China users skirt ban', www.

bloomberg.com/news/2012-09-27/facebook-tops-63-million-users-in-china-despite-ban-report-says.html.

*Mail Online* (2008) 'Injured Oxford winger Deering fined by his club for racist attack on nurses who cared for him', 31 December, www.dailymail.co.uk/sport/football/article-1103609/Injured-Oxford-winger-Deering-fined-club-racist-attack-nurses.html.

*Mail Online* (2012) 'Black ice hockey player subjected to racist tweets after stunning overtime goal says they're "shocking, but didn't ruin my day"', 27 April, www.dailymail.co.uk/news/article-2136101/Joel-Ward-subjected-racist-tweets-stunning-overtime-goal.html.

Malik, K. (1996) *The Meaning of Race*, London: Macmillan.

Malik, S. (2002) *Representing Black Britain: Black and Asian Images on Television*, London: Sage.

Marchioro, K. (2001) 'From Sambo to Brute: the social construction of African American masculinity', *The Edwardsville Journal of Sociology*, 1, www.siue.edu/sociology/EJS/marchioro.htm.

Mason, D. (2000) *Race and Ethnicity in Modern Britain*, Oxford: Oxford University Press.

Mason, P. (2013) *Why It's Still Kicking Off Everywhere: The New Global Revolutions*, London: Verso.

McClendon, C. (1998) 'Cricket', http://postcolonialstudies.emory.edu/cricket/.

McDermott, M. and Jaffray, W. (2011) '#RiotWombles on the march: 200 rioters caused this mayhem … 500 offer help to clean up mess', www.dailymail.co.uk/news/article-2024035/UK-riots-2011-500-Londoners-offer-help-clean-rioters-mess.html.

McDonald, I. and Ugra, S. (1998) *Anyone for Cricket? Equal Opportunities and Changing Cricket Cultures in Essex and East London*, London: Centre for Sport Development Research.

McKee, H. (2002) '"YOUR VIEWS SHOWED TRUE IGNORANCE!!!": (Mis)Communication in an online interracial discussion forum', *Computers and Composition*, 19, 4: 411–434.

Meer, N. and Nayak, A. (2013) 'Race ends where? Race, racism and contemporary sociology', *Sociology E-special Issue 2*, http://soc.sagepub.com/content/early/2013/11/15/0038038513501943.full.

Memmi, A. (2009) 'Racism and difference', in Les Back and John Solomos (eds) *Theories of Race and Racism*, London: Routledge.

Miles, R. (1989) *Racism*, London: Routledge.

Mills, C. (2007) 'White ignorance', in S. Sullivan and N. Tuana (eds) *Race and Epistemologies of Ignorance*, Albany: State University of New York Press, 12–38.

Modood, T. (1994) *Changing Ethnic Identities*, London: PSI.

Modood, T. (1997) *Ethnic Minorities in Britain: Diversity and Disadvantage*, London: Policy Studies Institute.

Montagu, A. (1974) *Man's Most Dangerous Myth: The Fallacy of Race*, New York: Oxford University Press.

Morris, S. (2012) 'Student jailed for racist Fabrice Muamba tweets', *Guardian*, 27 March, www.guardian.co.uk/uk/2012/mar/27/student-jailed-fabrice-muamba-tweets.

Nakamura, L. (2002) *Cybertypes: Race, Ethnicity, and Identity on the Internet*, New York: Routledge.

Nakamura, L. (2008) *Digitizing Race: Visual Culture of the Internet*, Minnesota: Minnesota Press.

NBA Online (2009) 'NBA gets high marks for diversity in new study', 10 June, www.nba.com/2009/news/06/10/NBA.diversity.ap/.

Negroponte, N. (1995) *Being Digital*, New York: Vintage.

Omi, M. (1996) 'Racialization in the post-civil rights era', in Avery Gordon and Christopher Newfield (eds) *Mapping Multiculturalism*, Minneapolis: University of Minnesota Press, 178–186.

Omi, M. and Winant, H. (1986) *Racial Formation in the United States: From the 1960s to the 1980s*, New York: Routledge.

Omi, M. and Winant, H. (1994) *Racial Formation in the United States: From the 1960s to the 1990s*, London: Routledge.

Otis, J. (1993) *Upside Your Head!: Rhythm and Blues on Central Avenue*, Hanover: Wesleyan University Press.

Pandya, A. (2012) 'Twitter prosecutions: the CPS is attempting to deprive us of our liberty for the use of words', *Mail Online*, 28 March, www.dailymail.co.uk/debate/article-2121677/Liam-Stacey-Twitter-prosecution-The-CPS-attempting-deprive-liberty.html.

Pearce, C., Boellstorff, T. and Nardi, B.A. (2009) *Communities of Play: Emergent Cultures in Multiplayer Games and Virtual Worlds*, Cambridge, MA: The MIT Press.

PFA.com (2013) 'Social media: things to remember', www.thepfa.com/thepfa/socialmedia/thingstoremember.

Pilkington, A. (2003) *Racial Disadvantage and Ethnic Diversity in Britain*, Basingstoke: Palgrave Macmillan.

Plant, A.E. and Devine, P.G. (1998) 'Internal and external motivation to respond without prejudice', *Journal of Personality and Social Psychology*, 75, 3: 811–832.

Poole, E. (2002) *Reporting Islam: Media Representations of British Muslims*, London: I.B. Tauris.

Poole, E. and Richardson, J. (2006) *Muslims and the News Media*, London: I.B. Tauris.

Premier League (2012) 'Written evidence submitted by the Premier League to Culture, Media and Sport Committee – Racism in football', www.publications.parliament.uk/pa/cm201213/cmselect/cmcumeds/89/89vw12.htm.

Price, J., Farrington, N. and Hall, L. (2012) 'Tweeting with the enemy? The impacts of new social media on sports journalism', *Journalism Education*, 1, 1: 9–20.

Price, J., Farrington, N. and Hall, L. (2013a) 'Changing the game? The impacts of Twitter on relationships between football clubs, supporters and the sports media', *Soccer and Society*, 14, 4: 446–461.

Price, J., Farrington, N., Kilvington, D. and Saeed, A. (2013b) 'Black, white and read all over: institutional racism and the sports media', *International Journal of Sport and Society*, 3: 81–90.

Quantcast Online (2013) www.quantcast.com/twitter.com#!demo&anchor=panel-ETHNICITY.

Ratcliffe, P. (2004) *Race, Ethnicity and Difference: Imagining the Inclusive Society*, Maidenhead: Open University Press.

Reardon, S. (2012) 'Was the Arab spring really a facebook revolution?', www.

newscientist.com/article/mg21428596.400-was-the-arab-spring-really-a-facebook-revolution.html#.UwRYgfl_v7Y.

Rheingold, H. (2000) 'Rethinking virtual communities', *The Virtual Community: Homesteading on the Electronic Frontier*, revised edition, Cambridge, MA: MIT Press.

Richardson, J.E. (2004) *(Mis)Representing Islam: The Racism and Rhetoric of British Broadsheet Newspapers (Discourse Approaches to Politics, Society, and Culture)*, volume 9, Philadelphia, PA: John Benjamins Pub Co.

Riggins, S. (1997) *The Language and Politics of Exclusion: Others in Discourse*, London: Sage.

Rowe, D. (2004) *Sport, Culture and the Media*, second edition, Maidenhead: Open University Press.

Russo, M. (1997) 'NHL suspends Berube for slur', *Sun-Sentinel*, 26 November, http://articles.sun-sentinel.com/1997-11-26/sports/9711250726_1_racial-slur-worrell-racist-intent.

Saeed, A. (1999) 'The media and new racisms', *Media Education Journal*, December.

Saeed, A. (2003) 'What's in a name? Muhammad Ali and the politics of cultural identity', in A. Bernstein and N. Blain (eds) *Sport, Media, Culture: Global and Local Dimensions*, London: Frank Cass.

Saeed, A. (2004) '9/11 and the consequences for British-Muslims', in John Morland and David Carter (eds) *Anti-Capitalist Britain*, Manchester: New Clarion Press, 70–81.

Saeed, A. (2007) 'Media, racism and Islamophobia: the representation of Islam and Muslims in the media', *Sociology Compass*, 1, 2: 443–462.

Saeed, A. (2011) '9/11 and the increase in racism and Islamophobia: a personal reflection', *Radical History Review*, 210–215.

Saeed, A. (2014) 'Hip-hop Islam and woman', in Sarah Hackett and Geoff Nash (eds) *Postcolonial Islam*, London: Routledge.

Saeed, A., Blain, N. and Forbes, D. (1999) 'New ethnic and national questions in Scotland: post British identities among Glasgow-Pakistani teenagers', *Ethnic and Racial Studies*, 22, 5: 821–844.

Said, E.W. (1985) *Orientalism*, Harmondsworth: Peregrine.

Salih, R. (2004) 'The backward and the new: national, transnational and post-national Islam in Europe', *Journal of Ethnic and Migration Studies*, 30, 5: 995–1011.

Sears, D.O. (1988) 'Symbolic racism', in P. Katz and D. Taylor (eds) *Eliminating Racism: Profiles in Controversy*, New York: Plenum Press, 53–84.

Sharma, R. (2013) 'Next stop is Wembley Park! Germany stars stun commuters by taking the tube to training ahead of England showdown', *Mail Online*, 18 November, www.dailymail.co.uk/sport/worldcup2014/article-2509557/Germany-stars-Tube-Wembley-training-England-clash.html.

Shek, Y.L. (2006) 'Asian American masculinity: a review of the literature', *The Journal of Men's Studies*, 14, 3: 379–391.

Sherwell, P. (2013) 'US ethnic minorities make up 49.9 per cent of under-fives', *Telegraph*, 13 June, www.telegraph.co.uk/news/worldnews/northamerica/usa/10117951/US-ethnic-minorities-make-up-49.9-per-cent-of-under-fives.html.

Shirky, C. (2008) *Here Comes Everybody: The Power of Organizing without Organizations*, New York: Penguin.

Shirky, C. (2011) *Cognitive Surplus: Creativity and Generosity in a Connected Age*, London: Penguin.

Show Racism the Red Card (SRTRC) (2012) 'Written evidence submitted by Show Racism the Red Card to Culture, Media and Sport Committee – Racism in football', www.publications.parliament.uk/pa/cm201213/cmselect/cmcumeds/89/89vw02.htm.

Silver, D. (2000) 'Margins in the wires: looking for race, gender, and sexuality in the Blacksburg electronic village', in B. Kolko, L. Nakamura and G. Rodman (eds) *Race in Cyberspace*, London: Routledge.

Slot, O. (2007) 'Pakistan's World Cup failures weighed down by extra baggage on their return', *The Times*, 29 March, www.thetimes.co.uk/tto/sport/cricket/article2252412.ece.

Smart, N. (2013) 'Collingwood star Harry O'Brien says he lives with discrimination every day', *Herald Sun*, 30 May, www.heraldsun.com.au/sport/afl/collingwood-star-harry-obrien-says-he-lives-with-discrimination-every-day/story-fni5f6hd-1226653035604.

Smith, A. (2011) 'Twitter Update 2011', *Pew Research Internet Project*, 1 June, www.pewinternet.org/2011/06/01/twitter-update-2011/.

Smith, A. (2014) 'African Americans and technology use', *Pew Research Internet Project*, 6 January, www.pewinternet.org/2014/01/06/african-americans-and-technology-use/.

Smith, C. (2013) 'The planet's 24 largest social media sites, and where their next wave of growth will come from', *Business Insider*, 29 November, www.businessinsider.com/a-global-social-media-census-2013-10.

Smith, J. (2012) 'Jail is no place for mouthy drunks', *Independent*, 1 April, www.independent.co.uk/voices/commentators/joan-smith/joan-smith-jail-is-no-place-for-mouthy-drunks-ask-liam-stacey-7606078.html.

Solomos, J. (2003) *Race and Racism in Britain*, third edition, Basingstoke: Palgrave Macmillan.

St. Louis, B. (2004) 'Sport and common-sense racial science', *Leisure Studies*, 23, 1: 31–46.

Standage, T. (2013) *Writing on the Wall: Social Media, the First 2,000 Years*, New York: Bloomsbury.

Stangor, C. (2009) 'The study of stereotyping, prejudice and discrimination within social psychology', in Todd D. Nelson (ed.) *Handbook of Prejudice, Stereotyping and Discrimination*, New York: Taylor and Francis.

Steele, C.M. and Josephs, R.A. (1990) 'Alcohol myopia: its prized and dangerous effects', *American Psychologist*, 45, 8: 921–933.

Steele, C.M. and Southwick, L. (1985) 'Alcohol and social behaviour 1: the psychology of drunken excess', *Journal of Personal and Social Psychology*, 48, 1: 18–34.

Steiner, P (1993) "On the Internet nobody knows you're a dog" New Yorker 69:61.

Stephan, W.G. and Stephan, C.W. (1985) 'Intergroup anxiety', Journal of Social Issues, 41, 3: 157–175.

Sue, D., Capodilupo, C., Torino, G., Bucceri, J., Holder, A., Nadal, K. and Esquilin, M. (2007) 'Racial microaggressions in everyday life: implications for clinical practice', *American Psychologist*, 62, 4: 271–286.

Suler, J. (2004) 'The online disinhibition effect', *CyberPsychology & Behavior*, 7, 3: 321–326.

*Sun* (2013) 'Muamba Twitter troll is jailed', http://archive.today/sO9Qr.

Syal, R. (2001) 'Support England, Nasser tells young Asians', *Daily Telegraph*, 27 May, www.telegraph.co.uk/news/uknews/1331816/Support-England-Nasser-tells-young-Asians.html.

Tajfel, H. (1970) 'Aspects of ethnic and national loyalty', *Social Science Information*, 9: 119–144.

Tajfel, H. (1972) 'Social categorisation', in E. Moscovici (ed.) *Introduction A La Psychologie Sociale*, volume 1, Paris: Larousse.

Tajfel, H. (1973) 'The roots of prejudice: cognitive aspects', in P. Watson (ed.) *Psychology and Race*, London: Academic Press.

Tajfel, H. (1978) *The Social Psychology of Minorities*, New York: Minority Rights Group.

Tajfel, H. (1981) *Human Groups and Social Categories*, New York: Cambridge University Press.

Tajfel, H. and Turner, J.C. (1979) 'An integrative theory of intergroup conflict', in W.G. Austin and S. Worchel (eds) *The Social Psychology of Intergroup Relations*, Monterey, CA: Brooks-Cole.

Tajfel, H. and Wilkes, A.L. (1963) 'Classification and quantitative judgment', *British Journal of Psychology*, 54: 101–114.

Tajfel, H., Billig, M.G., Bundy, R.P. and Flament, C. (1971) 'Social categorization and intergroup behaviour', European Journal of Social Psychology, 1, 2: 149–178.

The Runnymede Trust (1997) *Islamophobia: A Challenge For Us All*, London: Runnymede Trust.

*The Sentinel* (2013) 'Facebook name Staffordshire Police a social networking "success story"', 25 November, www.stokesentinel.co.uk/Facebook-Staffordshire-Police-social-networking/story-20219039-detail/story.html#ixzz2posc1EEF.

*The Telegraph Online* (2012) 'England's code of conduct revealed: watch your tweets, ration the Xbox and ditch the headphones', 17 October, www.telegraph.co.uk/sport/football/teams/england/9614013/Englands-code-of-conduct-revealed-watch-your-tweets-ration-the-Xbox-and-ditch-the-headphones.html.

True Vision (2014) 'Internet hate crime', www.report-it.org.uk/reporting_internet_hate_crime.

Turkle, S. (1997) *Life on the Screen: Identity in the Age of the Internet*, New York: Simon & Schuster.

Van Dijck, J. (2013) *The Culture of Connectivity: A Critical History of Social Media*, Oxford: Oxford University Press.

Van Dijk, J. (2005) *The Deepening Divide: Inequality in the Information Society*, London: Sage.

Van Dijk, T. (1993) *Elite Discourse and Racism*, Newbury Park, CA: Sage.

Van Dijk, T. (1991) *Racism and the Press*, London: Sage.

Vera, H. and Feagin, J. (2004) 'The study of racist events', in M. Bulmer and J. Solomos (eds) *Researching Race and Racism*, London: Routledge, 66–77.

Vyas, R. (2008) 'What do they know of cricket who only cricket know?', www. hindu.com/lr/2008/01/06/stories/2008010650030200.htm.

Wainwright, M. (2012) 'Man who racially abused Stan Collymore on Twitter spared prison', *Guardian*, 21 March, www.guardian.co.uk/technology/2012/mar/21/man-racially-abused-collymore-twitter-spared-prison.

Walsh, R. (1985) 'Australia observed', *Daedalus*, 114, 1: 421–438.

Webb, J., Schirato, T. and Danaher, G. (2002) *Understanding Bourdieu*, London: Sage.

Wellman, D.T. (1977) *Portraits of White Racism*, Cambridge: Cambridge University Press.

Westall, C. (2012) 'Cricket, empire and the BBC', www.opendemocracy.net/ourbeeb/claire-westall/cricket-empire-and-bbc.

White, J. (2013) 'David "Bumble" Lloyd: I take cricket seriously, but not myself', *Telegraph*, 8 July, www.telegraph.co.uk/sport/cricket/international/theashes/10165375/David-Bumble-Lloyd-I-take-cricket-seriously-but-not-myself.html.

Wilder, D.A. (1986) 'Social categorization: implications for creation and reduction of intergroup bias', *Advances in Experimental Social Psychology*, 19: 291–355.

Williams, J. (2000) 'Asians, cricket and ethnic relations in northern England', *Sporting Traditions*, 16, 2: 39–53.

Wilson, E.J. and Costanza-Chock, S. (2012) 'New voices on the net? The digital journalism divide and the costs of network exclusion', in Lisa Nakamura and Peter A. Chow-White (eds) *Race After the Internet*, New York: Routledge.

Wise, T. (2002) 'A look at the myth of reverse racism', http://raceandhistory.com/selfnews/viewnews.cgi?newsid1024893033,80611.shtml.

Yar, M. (2013) *Cybercrime and Society*, London: Sage.

YouTube: www.youtube.com/yt/press/en-GB/statistics.html.

Zarate, M.A. (2009) 'Racism in the 21st century', in Todd D. Nelson (ed.) *Handbook of Prejudice, Stereotyping and Discrimination*, New York: Taylor and Francis.

Zeisberger, M. (2012) 'Racism in hockey exists on both sides of the border', *Weekes Media*, 27 April, www.weekesmedia.com/2012/04/27/racism-in-hockey-exists-on-both-sides-of-the-border/.

Zimbardo, P.G. (1969) 'The human choice: individuation, reason, and order vs. deindividuation, impulse, and chaos', in W.J. Arnold and D. Levine (eds) *Nebraska Symposium on Motivation*, Lincoln: University of Nebraska Press.

Zirin, D. (2012) 'Jeremy Lin and ESPN's "accidental" racism', *The Nation*, 19 February, www.thenation.com/blog/166382/jeremy-lin-and-espns-accidental-racism#.

# Index